THE GREEK TRAGEDY
IN NEW TRANSLATIONS

GENERAL EDITORS
Peter Burian and Alan Shapiro

EURIPIDES: Andromache

EURIPIDES

Andromache

Translated by
SUSAN STEWART
and
WESLEY D. SMITH

OXFORD
UNIVERSITY PRESS

2001

OXFORD
UNIVERSITY PRESS

Oxford   New York
Athens   Auckland   Bangkok   Bogotá   Buenos Aires   Cape Town
Chennai   Dar es Salaam   Delhi   Florence   Hong Kong   Istanbul   Karachi
Kolkata   Kuala Lumpur   Madrid   Melbourne   Mexico City   Mumbai
Nairobi   Paris   São Paulo   Shanghai   Singapore   Taipei   Tokyo   Toronto   Warsaw

and associated companies in
Berlin   Ibadan

Copyright © 2001 by Oxford University Press, Inc.

Published by Oxford University Press, Inc.
198 Madison Avenue, New York, New York 10016

Oxford is a registered trademark of Oxford University Press

Library of Congress Cataloging-in-Publication Data
Euripides.
[Andromache. English]
Euripides : Andromache / translated by Susan Stewart and Wesley D. Smith.
p.   cm. — (The Greek tragedy in new translations)
ISBN 0-19-512561-4 (pbk.)
1. Andromache (Legendary character)—Drama.   I. Title: Andromache.   II. Stewart,
Susan.   III. Smith, Wesley D., 1930–   IV. Title.   V. Series.
PA3975.A6 S73   2001   882'.01—dc21   00-048324

9 8 7 6 5 4 3 2 1
Printed in the United States of America

EDITORS' FOREWORD

"*The Greek Tragedy in New Translations* is based on the conviction that poets like Aeschylus, Sophocles, and Euripides can only be properly rendered by translators who are themselves poets. Scholars may, it is true, produce useful and perceptive versions. But our most urgent present need is for a *re-creation* of these plays—as though they had been written, freshly and greatly, by masters fully at home in the English of our own times."

With these words, the late William Arrowsmith announced the purpose of this series, and we intend to honor that purpose. As was true of most of the volumes that began to appear in the 1970s—first under Arrowsmith's editorship, later in association with Herbert Golder—those for which we bear editorial responsibility are products of close collaboration between poets and scholars. We believe (as Arrowsmith did) that the skills of both are required for the difficult and delicate task of transplanting these magnificent specimens of another culture into the soil of our own place and time, to do justice both to their deep differences from our patterns of thought and expression and to their palpable closeness to our most intimate concerns. Above all, we are eager to offer contemporary readers dramatic poems that convey as vividly and directly as possible the splendor of language, the complexity of image and idea, and the intensity of emotion of the originals. This entails, among much else, the recognition that the tragedies were meant for performance—as scripts for actors—to be sung and danced as well as spoken. It demands writing of inventiveness, clarity, musicality, and dramatic power. By such standards we ask that these translations be judged.

This series is also distinguished by its recognition of the need of nonspecialist readers for a critical introduction informed by the best recent scholarship, but written clearly and without condescension.

Each play is followed by notes designed not only to elucidate obscure references but also to mediate the conventions of the Athenian stage as well as those features of the Greek text that might otherwise go unnoticed. The notes are supplemented by a glossary of mythical and geographical terms that should make it possible to read the play without turning elsewhere for basic information. Stage directions are sufficiently ample to aid readers in imagining the action as they read. Our fondest hope, of course, is that these versions will be staged not only in the minds of their readers but also in the theaters to which, after so many centuries, they still belong.

A NOTE ON THE SERIES FORMAT

A series such as this requires a consistent format. Different translators, with individual voices and approaches to the material in hand, cannot be expected to develop a single coherent style for each of the three tragedians, much less make clear to modern readers that, despite the differences among the tragedians themselves, the plays share many conventions and a generic, or period, style. But they can at least share a common format and provide similar forms of guidance to the reader.

1. *Spelling of Greek names*

Orthography is one area of difference among the translations that requires a brief explanation. Historically, it has been common practice to use Latinized forms of Greek names when bringing them into English. Thus, for example, Oedipus (not Oidipous) and Clytemnestra (not Klutaimestra) are customary in English. Recently, however, many translators have moved toward more precise transliteration, which has the advantage of presenting the names as both Greek and new, instead of Roman and neoclassical importations into English. In the case of so familiar a name as Oedipus, however, transliteration risks the appearance of pedantry or affectation. And in any case, perfect consistency cannot be expected in such matters. Readers will feel the same discomfort with "Athenai" as the chief city of Greece as they would with "Platon" as the author of the *Republic*.

The earlier volumes in this series adopted as a rule a "mixed" orthography in accordance with the considerations outlined above. The most familiar names retain their Latinate forms, the rest are transliterated; –os rather than Latin –us is adopted for the termination of masculine names, and Greek diphthongs (such as Iphigeneia for Latin Iphigenia) are retained. Some of the later volumes continue this practice, but where translators have preferred to use a more consistent practice of transliteration or Latinization, we have honored their wishes.

2. *Stage directions*

The ancient manuscripts of the Greek plays do not supply stage directions (though the ancient commentators often provide information rel-
evant to staging, delivery, "blocking," etc.). Hence stage directions must
be inferred from words and situations and our knowledge of Greek
theatrical conventions. At best this is a ticklish and uncertain proce-
dure. But it is surely preferable that good stage directions should be
provided by the translator than that readers should be left to their own
devices in visualizing action, gesture, and spectacle. Ancient tragedy
was austere and "distanced" by means of masks, which means that the
reader must not expect the detailed intimacy ("He shrugs and turns
wearily away," "She speaks with deliberate slowness, as though to em-
phasize the point," etc.) that characterizes stage directions in modern
naturalistic drama.

3. *Numbering of lines*

For the convenience of the reader who may wish to check the English
against the Greek text or vice versa, the lines have been numbered
according to both the Greek text and the translation. The lines of the
English translation have been numbered in multiples of ten, and these
numbers have been set in the right-hand margin. The notes that follow
the text have been keyed to the line numbers of the translation. The
(inclusive) Greek numeration will be found bracketed at the top of the
page. Readers will doubtless note that in many plays the English lines
outnumber the Greek, but they should not therefore conclude that the
translator has been unduly prolix. In most cases the reason is simply
that the translator has adopted the free-flowing norms of modern Anglo-
American prosody, with its brief-breath- and emphasis-determined
lines, and its habit of indicating cadence and caesuras by line length
and setting rather than by conventional punctuation. Other translators
have preferred to cast dialogue in more regular five-beat or six-beat
lines, and in these cases Greek and English numerations will tend to
converge.

Durham, N.C   PETER BURIAN
Chapel Hill, N.C.   ALAN SHAPIRO
2000

CONTENTS

ANDROMACHE

INTRODUCTION

Andromache is one of a number of Euripides' preserved plays that are concerned with distressed women. In *Alcestis*, the title character gives her life for her unworthy husband; in *Medea*, the heroine, because her husband betrayed her, kills their shared children; in *Hippolytus*, Phaedra destroys her beloved when he scorns her; and in *Hecuba*, the queen of defeated Troy takes an ugly vengeance on the murderer of her son. Each play has its own logic, but Euripides shows an overall tendency to bring into question, or even to parody, the conventions of heroic literature, which began with the *Iliad*. Alcestis and Medea achieve heroic stature while their husbands are presented as less than noble, men to whom honor means less than winning by whatever means. The heroes may speak as though they are in the mold of Achilles of the *Iliad*, but their actions belie it. The *Andromache*, along with *Hecuba* and *Trojan Women*, make a group that dramatizes the aftermath of the Trojan War from the point of view of the war's devastating consequences for its victims, especially women. These dramas are not inspired by heroic victory over a worthy foe or tragic failure in the attempt, though such values are still remembered. In *Andromache*, the poet contrasts heroic female qualities with unheroic male qualities. Hector's widow struggles to save her own life and that of her child from the callous vindictiveness of the Greek general Menelaus, who lacks a sense of honor. Menelaus is only an agent of his daughter Hermione in what she would like to think of as a contest in which she is upholding the ideals of Greek womanhood against the barbarian usurper. But in the conflict between the two women Euripides uses language and emphases that tend toward psychological realism, and the values at issue turn out to be not the old heroic values, but social and domestic ones.

In creating *Andromache*, Euripides picked an out-of-the-way part of

the mythology of the heroic period, and worked out its dramatic pos-
sibilities by altering and shaping the facts of the story in his own way.
We can see what it was in the subject that attracted the poet if we
notice the potentialities he brings out in his version. Immediately we
are struck by the way Andromache's life story lends itself to expression
of pathos: she began in innocence and in the happiest of circumstances, she devoted herself to doing the correct things as her circumstances dictated, and in the end she was brought down to the utterest
misery, finally to offer her own life to save her child's, but in vain,
since her torturer lied to her. Euripides sets up a series of moments in
which Andromache tells parts of her story, and he gives the chorus
lyric musings that support it with reminiscences of the causes and consequences of the Trojan War. Throughout, Euripides presents Andromache as a mature woman of dignity and heroism, the best of women
in the worst of circumstances. Behind or beside this portrait Euripides
has given himself scope to picture the culture that produced it. Andromache is a victim because as a woman she faces another more
powerfully placed woman's irrational jealousy. She is a victim because
war brought her own culture down, a war like other wars, fought with
talk of honor and shame, but fought by shameless people like Menelaus, themselves exceedingly limited.

Persistently Euripides draws our attention to woman's fate, woman's
nature. And persistently he flashes back and forth between the small
and the grand, the domestic and the national and international, the
personal and the universal. Menelaus' bad judgments in running his
household led to a gathering of Greek forces for an attack on Troy.
And in Troy, also, bad judgment had prevented their heading off the
actions that they could see would lead to disaster. In Neoptolemus'
house, divided control (two wives, which everyone talks about) has
caused disastrous turmoil that in the end destroys dynasties. But one
consolation is that a new dynasty is created in Molossia.

Such emphases and choices by the poet ask us to look further at the
way the play is organized to affect its audience. Two particular aspects
of the play have drawn much negative comment through the years: the
dramatic structure and the political overtones. I would like to talk about
them first, because judgments about them have broad implications for
the way we think about *Andromache* or any Euripidean tragedy. *Andromache*'s structure has been faulted because she, the heroine, and
with her the interest she brought to the play, virtually vanish about
halfway through. Those who are certain that this is a flaw see it as
symptomatic of the author's basic misunderstanding of how a play
should work. Other Greek tragedies, besides those of Euripides, have

anomalous structures. The term "diptych" has been much used in discussions of the change of dramatic focus in Sophocles' *Ajax*, for example. Critical literature abounds with assessment of the seriousness of such flaws, assessments inevitably connected to the importance of Aristotle's insights in the *Poetics*, and to questions of what dramatic unity might be if it is not focused on an individual's reversal of fortune.[1] Such discussions are not unimportant, but they only become cogent after they escape from the easy assumption that there is one best structure for drama, that all dramas should be judged against it, and it is a structure organized for maximum emotional impact at a climax. Many people are willing to contemplate and try to respond to other kinds of structures. It is for such people that Euripides wrote. Hence, without defensiveness, let us look at the way Euripides put *Andromache* together.

Andromache's structure is linear and sequential. The opening of the play portrays a crisis, Andromache's severe danger, and in a series of scenes she is brought to the verge of death and then rescued. At this point in the action the audience is engaged by another problem: Hermione's fear of punishment for what she has tried to do. Her fear is not unreasonable, and has in some sense been anticipated earlier. Neoptolemus' likely reaction was talked about, but the audience was not prepared for a second movement that would explore Hermione's problem. The long scene that dramatizes Hermione's "crisis" produces information about another impending crisis: the slaughter of Neoptolemus. Again, it comes out of the play's action, and in the event seems inevitable, but the audience was not earlier told to anticipate that that was the way things would move. Neoptolemus' slaughter does occur, and is described movingly. Following that, attention shifts to Peleus' utter grief, but then Thetis intervenes to offer reassurance, and a prediction of everyone's future.

Initially in the play, *Andromache*'s action provides a focused structure, with a beginning, middle, and end, a change of fortune, and so on, perhaps even a purgation of pity and fear, but following Peleus's entrance and Menelaus's withdrawal the audience's involvement in subsequent events is less emotionally intense, somewhat more detached and intellectual. One can say that surprise rather than suspense is what the audience is treated to. The audience is not so much moved by Hermione's difficulties as made uncomfortable. They cannot but be

---

1. Approaches to modern as well as ancient dramas assess them according to their matching a formula: is the play about a good person, does his fortune change, does it produce a "catharsis" of pity and fear, and so on. This is a hard mental rut to climb out of, if climbing out is needed, as I believe.

affected by her desperation, but at the same time they must be amused or bemused by the difficult position she has put herself in when her ruthless scheme fails. I think that it is fair to say that Euripides addresses the critical mind more than the emotion. We can appreciate this, I think, without needing to wonder whether he is making a comic or tragic structure. The wit and irony are essential to what Euripides did when he wrote tragedy. And without the earlier "tragic" action of the play, the later part would not work. In a comparable way, although the fate of Neoptolemus is dramatized for us in a vivid speech whose effect on Peleus the audience observes and feels for, the empathy with him is less intense and immediate than it was with Andromache in the early part of the play. The audience never knows Neoptolemus, and his fate allows a detachment that lets their minds appreciate the human and divine forces at play. In the compressed drama of Neoptolemus' death there is heroic confrontation of man and god, but the setting is sinister and the cause of what happens is ambiguous. Thetis' epilogue solves every problem and ties all details together, and in the process permits our savoring different kinds of satisfaction from the different parts of the drama, as Aristotle might say.

The second most common criticism of the play is that it depends for its effect on the cheap propaganda device of abusing the Spartans, against whom Athens was waging war. Once again, this is not a trivial question. It springs from a consideration of what tragedy ought to be, but it can be pursued in ill considered ways.[2] I think all readers must agree that Euripides plays on anti-Spartan sentiments. He expects some of the lines in the play to be effective because they touch the audience's feelings that have been roused by Athens' current danger from and hostility to Sparta. Importantly those feelings include personal fear, the sense that Athens could be destroyed, her people slaughtered and enslaved if Sparta has her way. Aside from the various remarks about Spartan treachery and cruelty, the telling jab comes at Menelaus' last departure from the stage. He has been faced down by Peleus, prevented from murdering woman and child, but he saves face by blustering that he has to leave to go home to punish and enslave a town near Sparta that has offended him, after which he will return to take care of things in Phthia in a heart to heart talk with his son-in-law. What Menelaus says is in no way out of dramatic character for him, whose treachery and casual cruelty have been successfully drawn in the action. But at this point, when the focus suddenly changes from the personal to the international, it offers a frisson of fear to the Athenian audience. We do not know the date of the *Andromache,* so we cannot know whether what Menelaus says may have reminded the original audience of a specific recent Spartan action against a neighbor, as it reminds modern students of Mantinea, which later suffered repeatedly from being Sparta's neighbor.[3] How appropriate, then, is Euripides' appeal to anti-Spartan sentiment? To my mind Euripides has used it all well, taking the immediate and turning it into the abstract and eternal. The anti-Spartan sentiments work like other appeals to emotional values, Greek-barbarian, male-female, even war-peace, light-dark. I do not see that they are used illegitimately or in a way to confuse the audience's mind as to what the poet is doing. The Spartans in the play represent an attitude and kinds of behavior common in Classical Greece, but common, too, in the heroic period. Nothing is made false by drawing a comparison between past and present, and the action of the play cannot by any stretch be read as current events wearing the mask of antiquity. The play's greatest anachronism occurs, I think, in Peleus' tirade on the bad bringing up of Spartan women to be immodest athletes, which translates later practices back into the bronze age, and accomplishes nothing by suggesting that Helen and Hermione were athletes.

Perhaps the actual driving issue, what it is that leads some people to a suspicion that there is an illegitimate emotional appeal to the audience, is the fact that the action of *Andromache* is drawn with broad strokes and may seem excessively melodramatic and black and white: the innocent noble woman and her boy are victimized by unfeeling powerful people and saved by the aura of a feeble but worthy old man. It is true that the tone approaches that of melodrama, and that the utter insensitivity of the Spartans contributes to that tone. Each of us has to judge whether such a play is tolerable, and if so, why. For me it succeeds because Euripides' characteristic irony tempers the melodramatic tone, as do his poetry and his wide range of intellectual subject matter. That is to say, Euripides does not reduce our area of consideration, as we think of melodrama doing, but goes from simple melodramatic form to increasing complexity of thought and emotion. One structural technique he uses for this purpose is worth noting: the dramatic stage action is so contrived as to promise immediate action, e.g., Andromache is about to be moved violently from her sanctuary, Menelaus drags her

---

3. It is a mistake to leap from Euripides' "abuse of Sparta" to say that this is a "patriotic play," differing in that respect from the later *Trojan Women,* which clearly expresses shame and indignation for Athens' brutality in the Peloponnesian war, and so is not "patriotic." Such categories are too reductive.

child in and is about to use violence to coerce her, Peleus and Menelaus face off when Menelaus refuses to release the bonds. The audience is riveted and ready, and the poet uses his riveting of the audience as a chance to explore ideas more extensively. A debate on women's needs and duties erupts between Hermione and Andromache, another debate on the role of reputation, on seeming versus being in human affairs occurs between Andromache and Menelaus, and later Peleus and Menelaus hold forth on the rival claims of family versus decency and honor. A powerful line each time sets the mental-verbal action going by elevating the immediate conflict to an expression of nature or culture (187f, 450ff, 697ff):

> A curse on mortals—that's what Youth brings us,
> and worst are the young without a sense of justice.

> Where's there a man who doesn't hate you Spartans—
> specialists in treachery, weavers of twisted intentions,
> captains of lies. . . .

> How senseless are the customs here in Greece.
> When armies raise their trophies over foes
> the crowd forgets the ordinary soldiers
> who did the work and suffered. Instead the general
> gets the laurels.

And this responds to (649ff):

> How can they say the old are wise? How did
> the Greeks speak of your good sense? . . . You made
> a marriage alliance with us and now you insult us. . . .

Thus, while the action is simple and can be called melodramatic, the poet engages us in such a way as to make us feel that the staged events are entwined with larger values and problems that he introduces. The play's setting, too, hints at essential human experience. The scene is set at a small temple in an insignificant place, but the scene itself touches in every member of the audience a core of fear, eliciting an attention that the poet can use to get his material in front of the audience. In the opening scene a suppliant clings to a statue of a goddess. The suppliant posture is one of helplessness, resignation, desperation at having passed beyond human help. Clothing and headdress (possibly shaved head) add to the pathos of the suppliant's position. The audience readily knows the meaning of the scene, and has feeling for the suppliant: many of those watching the play will have fled for their own lives and sought sanctuary at some time. All of them knew people who had. And a number of those in the audience might have been the pursuers in such events, and would have their own complex responses. Thus, while the setting of the play is in the mists of antiquity, in the heroic age, the action involved is so near as to be gripping. Even in civilized fifth century Greece, and even in Athens, the most civilized of cities, one depended on the gods for safety. The gods, most people believed, watched over their worshippers and their institutions. In times of desperation they were the only protection, and one became their suppliant in the hope that respect or fear for the gods would be effective. Fear of the gods often did restrain people from violence, but not invariably. Respect for the ritual of suppliance was increased by many stories of the curses that had pursued and ruined people who had violated the gods' sanctuaries. In myth the gods are generally very jealous of their prerogatives and their dignity. They are very likely to fly off the handle when crossed. They are very dangerous beings. The chorus's questions at 1012ff bring this out, as does, possibly, Apollo's response to Neoptolemus. What then should we make of divinity's function in this play? What becomes of the aura of holiness with which the play begins?

That the object of supplication is the goddess Thetis is told by Andromache in her opening speech. Thetis is not a major goddess, not commonly worshipped in Athens. She is fairly far off and misty. One knows her from the *Iliad* as a sea nymph most distressed by the tragic situation of her son Achilles. But the normal Greek was quite conscious that gods of any rank exercise great power in the vicinity of their own shrines where they are worshipped. As the scene develops, it is clear that Hermione and Menelaus are afraid to violate the sanctuary of Thetis' temple, despite their threats to burn it down and their bold assertions that they have no fear. On the whole it was safer to be afraid of the gods. But after Andromache is tricked into leaving the temple, the sense of Thetis' involvement fades into background both for the audience and the characters. Still, as it turns out, Andromache is saved by an old and weak man, and Thetis appears at the end to assert her authority and to take responsibility for everyone's future. The audience is free to feel Thetis' influence throughout the action as much as they desire. The play gives a simple shape: she was supplicated and she answered. The promise implicitly given by the stage setting is fulfilled.

Apollo similarly exercises power in the vicinity of his shrine. Neoptolemus goes to Delphi to apologize to Apollo, presumably to try to avert whatever malign influence Apollo might continue to exert on his life. When the messenger tells us what happened, he concentrates on what the Phthians saw in Delphi, and what they surmised from it. It is the mob of Delphians, urged on by Orestes, who are the agents of Neoptolemus' death, and they were egged on by gossip, innuendo, and slander. But one moment of divine mystery occurs during the battle in the temple, when it appears that the heroic and violent Neoptolemus of myth has risen to the occasion with his Pyrrhic leap and is going to beat his attackers. A profound voice sounds out from the temple, stunning Neoptolemus and rousing his attackers. The audience is again left to interpret the god's action as they wish.[4] I suspect that Sophocles or Aeschylus would have constrained the audience more directly, guiding their interpretation. Euripides tends always toward ambiguity in such matters, leading critics into many disputes about his attitudes. But here in *Andromache* the messenger helps us out somewhat. Though he has described all the mob's action and motivation in human terms relating to Orestes' schemes, he says at the end (1162ff),

> This is how the god who prophesies for all,
> who judges morality for all mankind, has treated
> the son of Achilles when he came to make amends.
> Like a cowardly man, he brooded on
> old quarrels—how can we call that wise?

Questions of belief deal not with atheism versus belief in the gods' existence, but rather with the nature and character of the gods.

The chorus directs a question to Apollo when they are trying to trace the chain of bad events. They want to know how Apollo and Poseidon could have turned against Troy, their own creation, and destroyed it along with the people they had protected. It is something of a rhetorical question, because the chorus are implying that there can be no adequate reasons. Similar feelings are produced by the chorus' retelling the story of the contest of the three goddesses and the judgment of Paris. Indeed, when looked at mythologically, the whole sequence of events, beginning with Helen's adultery and ending in the plight of Andromache, was caused by arbitrary, frivolous acts by divinities. So, the human action is played out before a background of superhuman entities. If such entities were submitted to the audience's discussion and judgment, widely different views would be expressed. Nor will we ever know the poet's views. Within the play, however, the dramatic effect of reference to the supernatural behind the event is to promote a sense of unity and completeness.

In so using divinities Euripides is continuing Greek literary traditions

---

4. The audience might well be reminded of Apollo's intervention in the battle in the *Iliad*, in which he stunned Patroclus and knocked him to the ground, where all could stab him.

as old as literature itself. In storytelling, in hymns to the gods, songs of praise for mortals, as well as in graphic arts, there is a tendency to weave divinity into the fabric of everything, and to trace events back to their divine sources. Even if events are adequately accounted for without the gods, the signs of the gods are said to be there anyway. The Greek artists have wide latitude in their use of such material, and need not even be self-consistent unless they wish.

In the foreground of the *Andromache* are human motive and action, and insistently our attention is drawn to women's nature, women's role, and so on, as it seems Euripides takes every opportunity to raise the topic and to introduce broad generalizations: love is the most important thing to a woman; woman is very jealous, and a bad woman is worse than a viper; they say a woman takes pleasure in rehearsing her miseries; she can always find an excuse for something. And the chorus sounds as though they are taking material from Aristophanes' comedies when they caution Hermione that women should stick together and cover one another's faults with cosmetics. There is a dose of irony in what Hermione says to elicit that admonition from the chorus. Hermione has proceeded from remorse and fear about the consequences of her brutality to Andromache and Molossus to a process of excusing herself. How could she have gone so wrong, she asks, and she concludes that the fault must lie with women, her women visitors to whom she confided her problems, and who gave her dreadful advice that led to her crimes. She declares that men should isolate their wives from other women and restrict their visitors because the society of women is dangerous. Hermione's simplistic reduction, along with instant social philosophy that presents an extreme version of the point of view that actually determined the status of women in classical Athens, is what I speak of as exemplary Euripidean irony. It seems indubitable, considering the amount and variety of attention he gives to it, that not only was Euripides interested in the status of women, but also that he wanted to draw the audience's attention to it. Ancient suggestions in Aristophanes' plays that Euripides was misogynist or feminist make sense in the light of such concentration. But we are forced to ask whether either label applies, and how do we prove it?

It is not easy to peer into a culture as alien to us as that of ancient Athens to see and judge sympathetically the subject of woman's condition, or to make out what is being said about it. The Greeks sometimes seem much like us, as when Andromache says "All men love their children." But we quickly learn that we cannot transfer values one by one, or make one for one equivalencies for meanings of words. It is well to remember the funeral speech Thucydides attributes to

Pericles at the end of the first year of fighting in the Pelopponesian War, in which, after giving a picture of Athens as the most enlightened and humane city on earth to that time, and after urging sons and brothers of the dead to carry forward the city's excellence, he turned to the women present: "If I must say anything on the subject of female excellence to those of you who will now be in widowhood, it will all be comprised in this brief exhortation. Great will be your glory in not falling short of your natural character; and greatest will be hers who is least talked of among the men for good or for bad."[5] The fact that Thucydides found that exemplary sentiment appropriate at such a symbolically important time cautions us against simple anachronistic judgments.

The society was patriarchal; women were largely sequestered, they were under the control and protection of the oldest male relative, who arranged their marriages and gave them dowries, and to whose protection they would revert if they were divorced. The woman was under effective control of her husband. There were a few legal limits to the abuse he could visit on her. Custom and public opinion offered the greatest restraints. All these things are alluded to in the play, whose family arrangements are like those of the classical period in which it was written.[6] And yet Euripides shows a delicate sympathy not only for the fallen aristocrat whose status deprives her of all rights, but also for the "fellow slave" who is sent into danger of death for Andromache's sake, and who says, "the life of a woman who is a slave has little value."

In the clash between Andromache and Hermione, Euripides divides woman's role into two to make the sharp contrast. Andromache is a wholly sympathetic figure whose point of view is well established before Hermione appears. In poignant antitheses between what she strove for and what she experienced, Euripides works on the themes that he used again in his portrait of Andromache in *Trojan Women* some years later.

> I aimed always at the prize
> all good women win, and my success
> won me ruin. All the modesty
> wit has conjured for us I pursued.
> First, the worst thing that we face,
> gossip, good or bad, when we go out,
> I avoided. I stayed within my home,
> I was not a shrew, nor coy nor shrewd.

5. From the translation of Richard Crawley.

6. I think the audience might have wondered, when Hermione says Neoptolemus will kill her outright on his return, whether that is something Euripides attributes to the more brutal heroic age in which the play is set, or whether she exaggerates in her hysteria.

My happiness was knowing where to stop.
Silence, and my eyes at peace on him.
When to win and when to yield I knew.
News of me spread to the Grecian camp,
so when Troy fell and we women became loot
I was first prize. Achilles' son chose me.
Son of the man who killed my husband, he
killed my husband's father. I am his.
His. Do I now push away the head
of Hector where it left its impress here?

As a type of perfect woman she is victimized by her own nature when she becomes the mate of a new owner. Hermione does not have such difficulties. And her problem as it is presented is that she is too assertive of her own wants and needs instead of most interested in what will be convenient and pleasing to her husband. She demands too much love, too much attention, too much eleutherostomia, the right to speak her will. But Hermione says that her view is the view of the civilized Greek. She is made to seem ridiculous when she imagines that Andromache's magic potions are ruining her, when she asserts that the barbarian will not play fair because her type of people can put up with any indignity, including incest. But Andromache brings us up somewhat short when she says (225ff),

O dearest Hector, for your sake, I opened
my heart to your loves when Cypris caught you.
I often served as wet-nurse, offering my breasts
to your bastards, to show you I was not bitter.
And with such wifely perfection, I led you to love me.

Earlier Euripides has Andromache argue that if a woman marries into a Thracian house where there are many wives, she should govern her passions accordingly. Thus, in the same way as Euripides pulls out the stops in his treatment of Hermione as the young and selfish, snobbish, Spartan girl, in whom the normal passions of a young wife turn murderous, he also tweaks the audience when he draws the portrait of the ideal submissive woman and wife. Yes, those barbarians are a bit extreme, perhaps. It seems that Euripides is not really proposing an answer to questions about the "woman problem" in his culture so much as using the elements of it to heighten sensitivity. Or perhaps a better analysis can produce a different answer.

The chorus in *Andromache* is women from Phthia. They feel closer to Andromache than to Hermione because she lives in Phthia, and because they can empathize with her powerlessness. They are simple, no-nonsense, moral Greek women. Hence they mediate between the audience and the players on stage. They are loyal to the house of Aeacus, to the memory of Achilles, and to Neoptolemus. They feel and respond to the innocence of Andromache and Molossus, the high-strung selfishness of Hermione, the insensitive cowardly bluster of Menelaus, the aged dignity and goodness of Peleus, and so on. They think and feel in their own character for the most part. The chorus is there to say a few things in dialogue but primarily to contribute to the lyric, musical portion of the play. Unfortunately, with the loss of the music and all but a few vague descriptions of the dance, we cannot really get at its effect, but must take it on faith that it enhanced the drama considerably. The lyric passages sung by the chorus keep returning to the Trojan story, to the judgment of Paris on the three goddesses, to Poseidon and Apollo's vengeance on Troy, and the chorus tends to conventional views. They extol nobility, with Peleus as the example, and deprecate divided authority, in Neoptolemus' house and elsewhere. At the end they sing the refrain Euripides also used elsewhere, which boils down to "What happens is not what you expect will happen," or, as A. E. Housman put it in his parody of Greek tragedy, "Life is uncertain."

The chorus does not speak for the poet or characters. Its tag at the end of the play is one of a number of examples of irony or understatement by the poet. If the play does, in the end, produce a sense of unity as well as of rightness and therefore of inevitability, it is because Euripides, who Aristotle said is "the most tragic of the poets," is actually the most realistic of the Athenian tragedians in spite of all his fancies and diversions. At the end of *Andromache* Thetis sets all right, but leaves Neoptolemus dead, leaves Hermione, Menelaus, and Orestes as we saw them. And, of course, the realities that Euripides has pointed out to his audience are all in place, including the rituals of war and man's inhumanity. Despite the superficially cheerful conclusion, the view of life that Euripides presents in *Andromache*, as in all his work, is fundamentally tragic.

Philadelphia, Pa.   WESLEY D. SMITH
2001

ANDROMACHE

Characters

ANDROMACHE slave and concubine of Neoptolemus, a Trojan woman, widow of Hector

MAIDSERVANT an enslaved Trojan woman

CHORUS of Phthian women

HERMIONE Spartan princess, wife of Neoptolemus, daughter of Helen and Menelaus.

MENELAUS King of Sparta

MOLOSSUS son of Andromache

PELEUS father of Achilles, grandfather of Neoptolemus

NURSE of Hermione

ORESTES nephew of Menelaus

MESSENGER

THETIS goddess, once wife of Peleus

Line numbers in the right-hand margin of the text refer to the English translation only, and the Notes on the Text at p. 57 are keyed to these lines. The bracketed line numbers in the running head lines refer to the Greek text.

The scene is the temple of THETIS, *near the front of Neoptolemus' palace in Phthia.*
The temple is an open structure with an altar in front, stairs up to the peristyle, and
a statue of THETIS *visible on a pedestal inside.* ANDROMACHE *is sagging in front of the*
statue, clinging to its knees in a posture of suppliance. She rises and speaks, while
moving about the shrine.

ANDROMACHE Glory of all Asia, city of Thebe,
　　　　　　　from you in that far time, I came dowered
　　　　　　　with bridal gold to Priam's royal hearth.
　　　　　　　I, Andromache, came as the true-wed
　　　　　　　wife of Hector, the one who would give the world
　　　　　　　his sons. Andromache, so worthy of envy.
　　　　　　　But now I am the most miserable of women.
　　　　　　　I saw Hector, my husband, slain by Achilles.
　　　　　　　I saw Astyanax, the son I bore,
　　　　　　　hurled from the highest ramparts—murdered　　　　　　　10
　　　　　　　as the Greeks seized the hill of Troy.
　　　　　　　And I, a child of the freest of all houses,
　　　　　　　was brought as a slave to the shores of Hellas
　　　　　　　and given as the choicest spoil of war
　　　　　　　to the islander Neoptolemus.
　　　　　　　Now I live near the town of Pharsalia on the plains
　　　　　　　that border Phthia—lands where the sea goddess, Thetis,
　　　　　　　dwelled as the wife of Peleus, avoiding humankind.
　　　　　　　People in Thessaly, in memory of her marriage,
　　　　　　　call this place Thetideion.　　　　　　　　　　　　　20
　　　　　　　Achilles' son made his home in this place and honored
　　　　　　　Peleus's rule. As long as the old king lives,
　　　　　　　the grandson refuses the scepter. I myself
　　　　　　　have borne a son here, a son to Achilles' son,
　　　　　　　for he remains my master and I his slave.
　　　　　　　Before then I lived in misery. Yet, since his birth,
　　　　　　　hope has sustained me—the hope that, if he is saved,
　　　　　　　I'll find in him some succor and strength in my troubles.
　　　　　　　And since my lord wed the Spartan princess,
　　　　　　　Laconian Hermione, he spurns this slave's bed.　　　　30
　　　　　　　She, his bride, has cruelly wronged me, saying
　　　　　　　I've used secret potions to make her childless
　　　　　　　and thereby made her husband hate her.

She says I want to take her place as lady
of the house and force her from her husband.
But from the first I took his bed without
consenting. Now I have left it. Zeus is my witness.
I shared that bed against my will and heart.
She has no faith in what I say; she wants
to kill me and now her father, Menelaus,   40
has joined her to help destroy me. He's in the house.
He came from Sparta for that very purpose.
In fear, I have fled to Thetis's shrine,
she will protect me. Peleus and his descendents
revere this monument to his marriage with Thetis.
I have sent my only living son
in secret to another house, for here
he may be killed. His father is not near
enough to offer me protection, nor can
he help the boy. He has gone to Delphi   50
to atone for the madness he showed in the past
when, at Pytho, he demanded justice of Apollo,
for the god had killed his father, Achilles.
He hopes that, by begging forgiveness for his mistake,
he will come into the favor of the god.

Enter MAIDSERVANT.

MAIDSERVANT My queen, I do not hesitate to use that title
since I showed you the same respect in your own
home when we lived in Troy. I was loyal
to you and to your husband when he was alive.
Now I come to bring you awful news,   60
in fear that my masters will see me, but in pity for you.
You must take care against the horrors that Menelaus
and his daughter are planning against you and your child.

ANDROMACHE Dear, dear fellow slave; indeed you are
a fellow slave to me, who was once your queen
and now am fallen very low. What are they doing?
What murderous schemes are they weaving?

MAIDSERVANT Dear queen, they plan to kill your son this time;
the little boy you've hidden from their eyes.

ANDROMACHE Oh no, can it be true that she has learned he is in hiding—   70
whose voice, whose tongue, has told her? Is it done?
I am undone.

MAIDSERVANT I do not know, but with my own eyes I have seen
Menelaus leave the palace, bent to find the boy.

ANDROMACHE Undone, utterly. I am utterly undone. Those vultures,
twin vultures, will snatch and kill my little one while
his hope, the man he calls father, is still at Delphi.

MAIDSERVANT Yes, if he were here you would not suffer so.
But as it is, you are without friends.

ANDROMACHE And still there is no word that Peleus might come?

MAIDSERVANT Even if he came, he's much too old to help you.   80

ANDROMACHE Yet I have sent for him—not once, but many times.

MAIDSERVANT Do you really think that anyone here has carried a
message for you?

ANDROMACHE I see, now I see. Yet you—would you take the message?

MAIDSERVANT What excuse can I use for leaving my post so long?

ANDROMACHE You, too, are a woman—you could find many reasons.

MAIDSERVANT It is dangerous. Hermione keeps a constant watch.

ANDROMACHE When trouble comes, will you renounce your
former friends?

MAIDSERVANT Do not stain me with that reproach—I'll go.
I may meet with evil, but the life
of a woman who is a slave has little value.   90

Exit MAIDSERVANT.

ANDROMACHE Go then, and I will extend to heaven
                 the lamentations, the sobs and tears,
                 to which my life seems given over.
                 They say a woman rehearses her misery,
                 taking pleasure as it spills from her lips.
                 Yet I have not one, but many sources for my grief;
                 my native city razed, my bond to Hector broken,
                 and the bitter yoke of slavery
                 that fate has placed, so unjustly, upon me.
                 Never call any mortal blessed until   100
                 you see, in his last hour, his last day,
                 how he goes down into the world of death.

                                           [*Intoned, like a funeral dirge*]

                 Helen arrived as a bride brought by Paris to lofty and
                      steepbuilt
                 Troy, but she was a curse, like a fury upon us.
                 Because of her, War came from Greece, in a thousand
                      swift ships to destroy
                 you, Troy, and the son of the sea goddess Thetis
                 dragged Hector behind his chariot, dragged him
                      three times around
                 the walls, a corpse through the dust of the chariot's ruts.

                 I, myself, captured and led from my bed, out of my inner-
                      most chambers,
                 wrapped horrid slavery about my bowed head and
                      went down   110
                 to the sea, to the strand of my exile. Then fast flowed
                      the tears as I left my poor
                 city, my sanctum, my bed, and my husband, my love there
                 entombed in the dust. Oh destiny, anguish of destiny!
                      Why do I
                 still look up, up to the light, even now as Hermione's slave?
                 Hounded and harried without a respite, I have thrown
                      myself, a suppliant,
                 on Thetis's statue. My tears come unbidden like springs
                      from a rock.

                                           Enter CHORUS, 15 *women of Phthia.*

CHORUS Woman, how long you've stayed on the floor   *strophe*
        of Thetis's shrine, staying your ground.
        Though I am from Phthia, I have come to you,
        Asian woman. I hope that I   120
        might concoct a remedy for this raging
        quarrel that locks you and Hermione
        together in violent hatred.
        Achilles' son is the source of that hatred.
        Two wives share him, so two wives suffer.

        Know your fate. Reason through   *antistrophe*
        where evil circumstance has brought you.
        You are at war with your masters.
        You are a Trojan woman struggling
        against high-born Spartans.   130
        Leave this house of the sea goddess
        where sheep are received for slaying.
        You will gain nothing by wasting away
        in desperate fear of your rulers.
        Power comes down on you, and you
        are nothing. Why struggle?

        Come then, leave the Nereid's   *strophe*
        glorious shrine. Know yourself—
        most miserable of women,
        you are a slave, a servant   140
        in a foreign city where
        you never meet anyone
        you have known as a friend.

        Pity is what we feel for you,   *antistrophe*
        a Trojan slave in our master's house.
        Fear holds our tongues, but pity fills our eyes.
        We don't want the daughter of Zeus's
        daughter to see the pity we bring you.

                                        Enter HERMIONE

HERMIONE I have wreathed my hair with strands of gold and draped
          these dappled veils about me, but it is not   150
          thanks to the first fruits, the marriage gifts
          of my bridegroom or his father, that I make

such an entrance. It was my father,
Menelaus, who bestowed such finery—
and a rich dowry, too—all the license I need
to speak my mind. Here is what I say:
You, slave woman, brought by the spear,
you would love to throw me out and make my house
your own. I am hated by my husband
because of your potions. It's your fault my womb is now   160
withered and empty. Such curses are a specialty
of you Asian women. But I am going to stop it.
The Temple of the Nereid won't help you,
and neither will its sacred shrine and altar.
You are going to die—even if he tried,
no man or god could save you. Forget your past,
        your former
glory; skulk here on the ground, grovel at my knees,
dip a hand into my golden basins and sprinkle the water
of Achelous drop by drop from my golden ewers.
Know where you are on earth; there is no Hector here,   170
no Priam, no fabled gold. This is a Greek city.
You are so stupid, so mindless, you had the nerve
to go to bed with the son of the man who killed
        your husband—
and you bore the baby of the one who slew your kin.
Yet this, too, is the kind of thing you barbarians do.
The father lies down with his daughter, the son marries
his mother, the sister takes up with the brother,
and family squabbles are settled with blood.
You may have no rule of law, but keep
such customs to yourselves. We think   180
a man who teams up two wives is only asking
for trouble. Anyone who wants a happy home
will search for a single wedded love.

CHORUS Every woman's heart is prone to jealousy
        and there is no hate like hate for a rival.

ANDROMACHE Oh, oh
        A curse on mortals—that's what Youth brings us,
        and worst are the young without a sense of justice.
        Because I am a slave, I fear my words will
        be discounted. And though I have a just   190

position, I may be punished for winning the argument.
The high and mighty, the self-righteous—all hate
to hear the truth from those below them. Still, I
won't be condemned because I dropped my own case.
Tell me, young woman, what line of reasoning led me
to push you out of your legitimate marriage bed?
Is Sparta humbled by Troy's splendor?
Am I blessed with wealth and freedom?
Do I have a girl's ripe beauty?
Do my powerful friends and great city   200
support me as I dispossess you?
And all so I can bear my sons as slaves—
each one a wretched weight upon my wretched life?
If you have no children, those sons of mine are sure
to be exalted as Phthia's royal kings!
Oh, how the Greeks love me for Hector's sake!
Andromache the obscure—a Trojan nobody.
Not because of my drugs does your husband
hate you—it's just that you're not a pleasing companion.
This, too, is a love potion: not only beauty   210
but perfect virtue, too, can prove a charm in bed.
When you are irritated, you always say that Sparta
is a great place and Scyros nothing.

Points to HERMIONE's *dress and jewelry.*

Here in poor Phthia, you show off your riches.
For you Menelaus is above Achilles.
Such things your husband truly hates.
Even the lowliest of husbands deserves to be cherished
and not opposed. What if you had married a king of
snow-bound Thrace, where men take to their beds
in turn numerous wives? Would you have killed   220
the others? Would you have blamed it all upon
their appetite for bed? How becoming!
It's true we pine for love more than our husbands do,
but it's only decent to keep it to ourselves.
O dearest Hector, for your sake, I opened
my heart to your loves when Cypris caught you.
I often served as wet-nurse, offering my breasts
to your bastards, to show you I was not bitter.
And with such wifely perfection, I led you to love me.

But you—you are even jealous of   230
the rain that falls to touch your husband's face.
Don't try to outdo your mother's philandering,
because children with such mothers should run
in the opposite direction—if they have any sense.

CHORUS (to HERMIONE) Mistress, with all respect, please try
to find some way to get along with her.

HERMIONE Why do you preach to me and argue with me
as if you alone are sensible?

ANDROMACHE Well, you clearly aren't. Just listen to you now.

HERMIONE I hope I'll never show the kind of sense that you have.   240

ANDROMACHE You're young, and yet your talk has such a nasty streak.

HERMIONE But you don't talk—with action you hurt me.

ANDROMACHE Will you not bear the pain of love in silence?

HERMIONE Why should I? Love's all a woman has to live for.

ANDROMACHE But love is only all for those who use it well.

HERMIONE Your barbarian laws will not hold sway here.

ANDROMACHE Here or there—no difference—shame is simply shame.

HERMIONE A clever wit—too bad you have to die.

ANDROMACHE And do you see the eyes of Thetis turned on you?

HERMIONE Expressing how she hates your people—the killers
of Achilles?   250

ANDROMACHE Helen killed him, not I—Helen, your mother.

HERMIONE Do you intend to keep it up, to open all my wounds?

ANDROMACHE All right, I'll be silent. I hereby seal my lips.

HERMIONE   But wait, tell me one thing, the thing I came to ask you.

ANDROMACHE   I tell you that you lack the sense you need.

HERMIONE   Will you, are you going to, leave this shrine of Thetis?

ANDROMACHE   I'll leave if I might live: if death awaits, I'll stay.

HERMIONE   Your death is destined. And I'm not waiting for
                   my husband.

ANDROMACHE   Until he comes, I'll cling to life, I'll never trust you.

HERMIONE   I will set you on fire without a thought for your fate.   260

ANDROMACHE   Strike your fire, but don't forget the gods are watching.

HERMIONE   Then they will see your flesh torn apart in horrid wounds.

ANDROMACHE   Slash away, bloody her altar—the goddess will pursue you.

HERMIONE   Barbarian creature, half-savage and stubborn,
                   do you really defy death? I will unseat you.
                   I have a lure that will make you consent in the end.
                   But for now, I won't announce it; the event
                   itself will soon disclose my meaning. Keep your seat
                   like a statue, as if molten lead had soldered
                   you to that sticking place. I'll pry you loose before   270
                   Achilles' son, your trusted champion, comes.

                                             Exit HERMIONE.

ANDROMACHE   Yes, it's he that I trust! How strange that the gods
                   have given us antidotes for all venomous
                   snakes, but none have ever found a cure
                   for an evil woman, worse than the stings of vipers
                   or flames. Such poison are we to mankind.

CHORUS   It was the beginning of terrible sorrows   *strophe*
                   when the son of Maia and Zeus
                   went into the glen of Ida, leading
                   a lovely team of three—three   280

goddesses. Armed with their beauty
for the hateful contest, they came
to the shepherd's lonely hearth —   280
to that wild place, to the poor door
where the shepherd kept his solitude.

When they came among the branches   *antistrophe*
and leaves of the shadowed glen, they bathed
their shining bodies in the splashing
mountain spring. And then they stood
in radiance before the son of Priam,   290
vying as rivals with hot words.
Aphrodite snared him in deceit —
words sweet to hear, but fatal
for the Phrygian city,
fatal to the walls of Troy.

If only she who gave birth to this evil   *strophe*
had raised him overhead and thrown
him far away before he came
to Ida's slope. Cassandra cried out —
imploring the elders, she cried for his death.   300
Beside the laurel of prophecy she shouted
against the blight on Priam's city.
Whom did she not approach?

For then the women of Troy would never   *antistrophe*
have been harnessed to slavery's yoke.
And woman, you would still be living
within your royal house. Then
the Greeks would have escaped a decade
full of agony, and young spearmen
would not have struggled to the death around   310
the walls of Troy. No beds would be bereft
of lovers, no old men would be bereft of sons.

Enter MENELAUS, *with* ATTENDANTS, *bringing* MOLOSSUS.

MENELAUS I'm here. I brought your son, whom you hid secretly
from my daughter in a neighbor's house.
You seem to have hoped this statue would save you
while the neighbors could save the boy. But you

26

have been proved not half as astute as Menelaus.
If you don't leave this spot, we'll slit his throat.
His corpse in return for yours.
So mull it over—do you want to die   320
or do you want this boy slaughtered
for all the wrong you've done to me and mine?

ANDROMACHE Fame, bloated fame! How many thousand
worthless mortals have you puffed up in glory.
Any who have gained renown through truth
deserve their laurels. But those who win by fraud
or chance I dismiss. They deserve nothing.
It's hard to believe that you were the one who led
the troops of Greece and ruined Priam's Troy—
you, a weakling who does your little daughter's bidding—   330
now you enter the fray against a hapless slave,
breathing such fire and fury!
You're not worthy of Troy, nor she of you.
Successful men like you might seem to shine.
Yet within you're merely mortal—just richer.
The gleam of wealth bestows that power you have.
So Menelaus, let's reason together: let's
suppose I'm dead, that your daughter has killed me,
she'll never flee this murder's bloody consequences.
The people will blame you, too, as her accomplice—   340
necessity will chain you two together.

Or let's suppose, instead, I live. And if you
kill my son do you think his father
would take that death in stride? Troy does not
speak of him as unmanly. He will do
what should be done—things worthy of Peleus
and his own father, Achilles; he's sure
to throw your daughter from the house. Do you
then have a plan to marry her off again?
Will you say her virtue led her to leave   350
her husband? The facts will be known.
Who will marry her? Shall she live
with you for years—drying up, turning gray?
You poor man—don't you see
the catastrophe at hand? How many betrayals
of your daughter's bed would you prefer

rather than suffer what I describe?
Don't turn a trifle into a disaster.
We women might be given to extremes,
but why copy us? If I have filled your daughter   360
with poisons and made her barren, as she claims,
my judge should be your son-in-law. I won't flee
to altars. I'm willing to submit to his justice,
for if I've made him childless, he has an equal
grievance against me. That is the kind of person
I am—I affirm it. But as for you,
I fear your nature. Because of a woman's quarrel
before, in the end it was Troy that you destroyed.

CHORUS   You are a woman, speaking to a man: you have gone
                too far,
            your righteousness has overshot its mark.   370

MENELAUS Woman, it's true that these are merely trifles, true
            they're hardly fitting for a king—or Greece.
            But don't forget, when something claims one's heart
            the goal can grow as strong as taking Troy.
            I'm here to help my daughter. I consider it
            a very great matter to be robbed of one's mate.
            There's nothing worse a wife can ever suffer.
            To lose her husband is to lose her life.
            My son-in-law must rule over my slaves
            and my daughter, with my help, will rule   380
            over his: true friends like us hold everything
            in common; there is no place for private wealth.
            It's up to me to set this house in order:
            waiting is for the weak, not the wise.
            So stand and leave this sacred shrine of Thetis,
            for if you die, this boy will not be doomed.
            But if you refuse, and live, I will kill him.
            One of you must now submit to death.

ANDROMACHE How cruel a lottery you set before me,
              a choice between two lives—when winning wins   390
              me wretchedness and losing brings ill fate.
              Oh you who from small causes take grand actions,
              why are you killing me? For whose sake? What city
              have I betrayed? What child of yours have I killed?

What house have I set on fire? Against my will,
I mated with my master. And then you kill me,
not him who was the cause. You overlook
the source as you pursue the end you want.
All these evils! Such misery to me,
such suffering to my land. Why did I have to   400
be a mother and with that double the pain
I bear? Yet motherhood isn't my only burden;
I have other sorrows equal to my present sorrows.
I saw Hector dragged behind the wheels.
I saw Ilium wrapped in pitiless fire.
Yanked by my hair, I went, a slave, aboard
the Argive ships. And when I came to Phthia,
I was wed to Hector's murderers.
Why should I value life? What should I think of?
Shall I look to the past or to the present?   410
The last eye of my life is this one child
and those who have power are going to kill him, but they
will hold back in exchange for my wretched life.
At least if he is saved, I have hope
and if I don't die for him, I have shame.
Look—I now am leaving the shrine. I'm yours
to hack, bind, murder, strangle with a rope!
My child, your mother goes to join those
in Hades so you may live. Having survived,
remember your mother—and why I died. When you   420
kiss your father, when he lifts you in his arms,
tell him with your tears and words all that I've endured.
For all mankind, children are their very life.
The childless criticize the childbearers, and always feel
less pain, but their blessing is in truth a kind of curse.

ANDROMACHE *comes down the steps of the shrine.*

CHORUS What I hear awakes my pity; for sorrow stirs
the hearts of mortals, even the sorrow of strangers.
You, Menelaus, should reconcile your daughter and
this woman so she might have some relief from her pain.

MENELAUS Seize this woman, come and tie her hands;   430
she'll hardly want to hear the words I'll say.

An ATTENDANT *seizes her.*

I've caught you now; I've dangled the boy's life
like a lure to make you leave the holy altar.
I've led you straight into my waiting trap.
You can be sure of death; your fate's a fact.
But as for your son, my daughter will
decide whether he should live or die.
Go to the house now. I'll teach you, slave,
not to vent your rage against the free.

ANDROMACHE Fooled! Duped! Caught by treachery and deceit!   440

MENELAUS Go tell the world! It's true; I won't deny it.

ANDROMACHE On the banks of Eurotas, this is called cleverness?

MENELAUS Of course, just as in Troy, we believe in revenge.

ANDROMACHE Have the gods lost their divinity? Do you think there is
no justice?

MENELAUS When there is, I'll bear it. But I'm going to kill you.

ANDROMACHE And kill my little babe, too, my chick, torn from beneath
my wing?

MENELAUS Not I. His death will be my daughter's bidding.

ANDROMACHE My little boy, there is no reason to delay my lament.

MENELAUS It's true, he has little to hope for.

ANDROMACHE Where's there a man who doesn't hate you Spartans—   450
specialists in treachery, weavers of twisted intentions,
captains of lies, assassins, never a straight
and honest thought, never a sound judgment—
your prosperity in Greece is a crime in itself!
There is no evil you have not committed.
Your hands itch with greed and the urge to murder.
Your lips say one thing while your hearts plot another.
Damn you! Death is not the worst I fear.

I died before when Phrygia burned: I died
with my glorious husband who so often sent you,   460
a whimpering coward, back across the sand
to your ships. You're such a fierce
warrior now, standing up to a woman.
Kill me! Kill on! You and your daughter
will hear no pleas or flattery from me.
Now you rule in Sparta, but I ruled
once in Troy. Don't boast of my destruction.
Your turn to suffer will surely come.

> *As she speaks* MENELAUS *moves toward the exit, and*
> *the* ATTENDANTS *herd* ANDROMACHE *and* MOLOSSUS *out.*

CHORUS Never will I approve of any mortal   *strophe*
having two mates, never should sons   470
live with two mothers. Strife
and pain and hate will fill the house.
Let a husband be content with one
mate, one mate for one man,
and share the bed with no one else.

Neither in cities is a pair of rulers   *antistrophe*
ever easier to bear than one.
Suffering is piled upon suffering and civil
war comes to the citizens.
When a pair of craftsmen draft one   480
hymn, the muses always cause strife.

When blasting winds sweep sailors along,   *strophe*
then a pair of minds at the helm,
even a whole crew of skilled men,
are weaker than a lesser mind
in full control. Under one roof
and over the city, the power of one
man will make the right decisions.

The Spartan woman proves it, the general   *antistrophe*
Menelaus's daughter. Against   490
her rival, she breathed fire. She tried
to kill the poor Trojan woman and
her child. Strife and pain and hate,

godless graceless slaughter.
Such things, lady,
bring reversal and revenge.

Now indeed here's the mother and son
yoked together so tightly—devoted to death.
Poor, poor woman. And you, wretched boy,
you are dying because of your mother's   500
marriage, though you're blameless, you bear
no fault toward the kings.

> *Enter* MENELAUS, *then* ANDROMACHE, *bound, with* MOLOS-
> SUS *holding onto her skirt.* MENELAUS' ATTENDANTS *are
> guarding them. They go up to the altar in front of
> the temple.*

ANDROMACHE   Here I am, being dispatched   *strophe*
to death; my hands are bloody from
these knots, so tightly bound.

MOLOSSUS   Oh mother, mother, beneath
your wing, I, too, go
down to death.

ANDROMACHE   Lords of Phthia, this
is an unholy sacrifice.   510

MOLOSSUS   Oh father, come and help your family.

ANDROMACHE   Dear little one, you will lie below,
crushed against
my own cold breast.

MOLOSSUS   Mother, what will become of me?
You and I could not be more wretched.

MENELAUS   Go down to your deaths in the Underworld.
You come from a city I hate.
Your two deaths come from two votes:
I've delivered your sentence—my daughter demands   520
the immediate death of your son.
A mere fool would allow his enemies,

or the children of enemies, life
when revenge could protect his home from fear.

ANDROMACHE Oh husband, husband—if only you   *antistrophe*
could come to spare us with your hand
and spear—Oh son of Priam.

MOLOSSUS My poor mother, what spell
or song of mine can turn away our fate?

ANDROMACHE Plead with him, my boy.   530
Clutch his knees in supplication.

MOLOSSUS Please, sir, do not harm me.
Please let me go.

MENELAUS *prevents* MOLOSSUS *from clutching his knees.*

ANDROMACHE My eyes are full of tears; they will not stop—
This misery flows like a sunless spring
that sends its water down the smoothest rocks.

MOLOSSUS Oh misery, how much misery—and for how long
shall I have to suffer?

MENELAUS Do not bother to supplicate me.
I'm as hard as a sea-worn cliff,   540
as relentless as sea-borne waves.
I would help my own family without hesitation,
but you, boy, do not move me. Remember
I wasted the prime of my life fighting to capture
Troy and your mother. Don't cling to me, cling to her
as you set off for the Underworld.

CHORUS Yet look, Peleus is on his way,
hurrying his old legs as fast as he can.

Enter PELEUS, *attended by a young man and followed in
the background by two armed attendants.*

PELEUS (*speaking as he enters*)
You, especially you who oversee this killing,

tell me—What are you doing? What's the meaning   550
of this? What is the reason for the chaos in the house?
What are you doing executing without trial?
Menelaus, stop your unjust haste!

Speaking to his ATTENDANT.

And you, lead me on now quickly.
I have no time to waste. If only I could
regain my former strength. First, I'll send
this woman a fair wind to fill her sail.

Speaks to ANDROMACHE.

Tell me,
by what right did these men bind you and the boy
and take you away? The lamb and the ewe are being   560
slaughtered when your master and I are gone.

ANDROMACHE Just as you see, old father, these men
are taking my son and me away to die.
What is left to tell you? Not once, but many
times I sent my cries of help to you,
messenger after messenger. You must have heard
of the fury of his daughter and why
I'm doomed to die. Now they have torn me from
the altar of Thetis, mother of your noble son—
the goddess you adore and revere.   570
They took me off by force; they did not hold
a trial or wait for those who were absent.
They knew that I and this child were all alone.
They are about to kill him in his innocence,
along with unhappy me.

She approaches him, holding out her bound hands.

But I beg you,
old father—I fall at your knees, for I cannot
reach your dearest beard in supplication—
save me, in the name of the gods!
I'll die, disgraced and disgracing your family.   580

PELEUS I order you to loosen this woman's bonds,
release her hands or you will pay for this.

MENELAUS But I say don't, and I'm the one in charge;
it's up to me, for I rule over her.

PELEUS What? Have you come now to try to rule my house?
Isn't it enough to rule the Spartans?

MENELAUS I captured her and brought her as a slave from Troy.

PELEUS Yes, but my son's son took due possession of her
as his prize.

MENELAUS What's mine is his—and all that's his is mine.

PELEUS For you to do well by, not badly, not by murdering.   590

MENELAUS Face the facts: you'll never rescue her from my control.

PELEUS You face the fact that this staff will bloody your head!

MENELAUS Touch me and see what happens! Just come near me!

MENELAUS *retreats.*

PELEUS What? Now you, a coward descended from
cowards, claim
to be a man? Why should anyone esteem you?
You lost your wife to a mere Phrygian! You left
your house without a lock or guard; you thought
she was a faithful wife, when really she was
the world's most wanton! No Spartan girl,
no matter her intention, could ever be chaste.   600
Their thighs bared and tunics opened, they leave
their houses with young men to race and wrestle.
Such sporting is intolerable;
how could you be surprised such girls are lewd?
Why don't you ask Helen to explain it?
She left the proper family she shared with you
and went off as if in a marriage procession,

with a young husband to another country.
So for her sake you mustered the bands
of Greeks and led thousands into Troy?   610
You should have spat her out, not lifted a spear
once you found her faithless, and left her in Troy—
even paid her not to come back! But your mind
veered in another direction. You went ahead
and destroyed so many brave lives, you left
old women childless in their homes, you
snatched away the noble descendents of white-
haired fathers—I know, I am one of them!
I hold that you are the murderer of Achilles,
as if you had killed him yourself, while you alone   620
returned from Troy without a scratch—your gleaming
armor in its pretty case, the same as it was
when you left. I warned my grandson, when he wanted
to marry, not to ally himself to your house,
to avoid the foal of an unchaste filly. Such daughters
repeat their mothers' faults. Be careful, suitors,
to always choose the daughter of a good mother.
Yet there's more—there's the terrible outrage you wrought
against your brother, urging the senseless slaughter
of his daughter. Were you so afraid to lose your   630
worthless wife? Then Troy fell (Yes, I pursue you here, too),
Helen was in hand, but still you didn't kill her.
One look at her breasts, and you let go of your sword,
kissing, lapping at that traitorous bitch
overcome by Cypris—you vile coward!
And then you came to my grandson's house while he
was gone: you pillaged the place and began
the slaughter of this helpless woman and child.
This boy will cause great pain in your own home,
even if he's three times a bastard.   640
For a dry patch often bears better than rich soil,
and bastards often are superior to rightful sons.
Now take your daughter away from this house.
A marriage alliance with an excellent poor man is better
than a match with a rich bad man. You are a nothing.

CHORUS The smallest start leads the tongue to great quarrels.
        Because of this, wise men will be careful
        not to spark a fight with their kin.

MENELAUS How can they say the old are wise? How did
the Greeks speak of your good sense? You are   650
Peleus, the son of a noble father. You made
a marriage alliance with us and now you insult us,
disgracing yourself—all for the sake of a barbarian.
You should have cast her beyond the Nile, sent her
beyond the Phasis, and called on me for help.
She's from Asia, where the ground is strewn with
          the corpses
of fallen Greeks. She played her part in the death
of your son. Remember that Paris, the one
who killed Achilles, was the brother of Hector.
And she was Hector's wife. And yet you   660
share the same roof with her, you enter by
the same lintel; she even sits at your table.
You let her bear the children who are your worst
enemies. Yet when I, for your sake and mine,
want to kill her, you snatch her from my grasp.
But come on, think. There's no shame in thinking:
if my daughter never has children, while this woman
does—will you set her sons up as kings of Phthia,
letting barbarians rule over Greeks? Are you
going to tell me that by hating what is wrong   670
I lack judgment and you are full of common sense?
And now give some thought to this:
What if your daughter had married a fellow citizen
and suffered this treatment? Would you sit quiet?
I doubt it. But, defending a barbarian, you attack
          your kin.
When abused, both women and men feel the same.
When they are wronged, women will always grieve.
So will a husband with a corrupted wife.
But the man has great power in his own hands.
For the woman, action depends on her family and   680
relations. Is it not right for me to help my own?
You are the oldest of old men. When you mention
my generalship, you help my case.
The gods corrupted Helen—not her will.
But in the end it brought great good to Greece.
Before, the Greeks knew nothing of arms and battle.
In war they came into their manhood;
acquaintance teaches mortals all things.

If I held back from killing my wife when finally
I stood before her, I did the right thing.   690
And you, I can wish you had not killed Phocus.
I come back at you with good will, not anger.
You deal with what follows a loose tongue and temper;
I'll be rewarded for my foresight.

CHORUS   Stop these wild and foolish words.
         Stop or you will go down together.

PELEUS   How senseless are the customs here in Greece.
        When armies raise their trophies over foes
        the crowd forgets the ordinary soldiers
        who did the work and suffered. Instead the general   700
        gets the laurels. He brandished his one spear among
        countless thousands, did one man's work—no more—
        and gets the praise. Those self-important officials
        of the city, though nobodies themselves,
        look down on other men. But citizens
        with wit and nerve show far more wisdom.
        Just so, you and your brother sit swollen
        with pride when you think of your generalship at Troy.
        But you were lifted by those who suffered and died.
        You'll see that even Paris of Ida is no match   710
        for the hatred that Peleus bears toward you
        unless you leave this house at once—you
        and your barren daughter. My son will grab her
        by the hair and drag her from one room to another—
        that sterile heifer; she's decided that if she can't
        have children, she won't let anyone else have them.
        Just because her own womb is empty,
        do we have to cut the thread of generations?
        Stand back from that woman, you slaves.
           Show me anyone
        who plans to stop me as I untie her hands.   720
        Come, stand up so that I can. These shaking
        old hands will loosen these twisted and knotted thongs.
        You coward—look how you've disfigured her hands.
        Did you think you were roping a bull or a lion with this?
        Or maybe you thought she'd draw a sword and rout you?
        Come here, under my arms, little boy,

help me untie your mother's bonds. I'll bring
you up in Phthia the enemy of these people.
Take away their fame in battle, take away
their fame in war, you'll find them no better
    than nothing.   730

CHORUS Old men are unbridled and hard to control—
    their tempers can flare so quickly.

MENELAUS You are far too inclined to abuse.
    But here in Phthia I won't stupidly resort to using
    force and I won't have force brought against me.
    For now, I'm in something of a hurry
    and so I'm going home. There's a town—a city—
    near Sparta that used to be our friend and now
    is making trouble. When I go back, I want
    to march on them and put them under my heel again.   740
    And when I've put things as I want them there,
    I'll come back. I plan a man to man
    talk with my son-in-law; we'll work things out.
    If he punishes this woman and is reasonable
    toward us, he'll be treated in kind.
    But if he makes trouble, he'll be met with trouble.
    I'll match his every deed, blow for blow.
    I plan to ignore your own empty words.
    You are a walking shadow with a voice.
    You talk and talk, but have no power.   750

Exit MENELAUS.

PELEUS My child, lead on, stand here under my arms,
    and you, too, poor woman. You've endured a fierce
    storm, but here's a safe harbor, sheltered from the wind.

ANDROMACHE Old sir, may the gods forever bless you for saving
    my baby and me, his luckless mother. Make sure, though,
    we are not ambushed in this deserted place.
    Now along the empty road, they might
    attack and carry me off by force, for they know
    you are old and I am weak and the baby is helpless.
    Watch out—having got away, we might be caught.   760

PELEUS Shhh! No more of these womanish fears!
Go ahead; no one will touch you—and if anyone
does, he'll be sorry. For by the grace
of the gods I have a great army—cavalry and infantry—
in Phthia. I'm far more vigorous than you think.
Old as I am, my glance will set such a man
in a panic. A brave-hearted elder is more
than a match for many young men.
What use is being of vigorous frame to a coward?

                                        Exeunt.

CHORUS Better never to be born if you cannot   *strophe*   770
be born a great noble, with wealth
and a strong haven to shield you from pain.
For when suffering comes the nobly born
have no lack of resources. There's always
a voice to proclaim the most famous,
to honor the glory of noble descendents.
For time will never wear away
the traces of their honor,
nor obscure the remains of their deeds.
Even in death, from the torches on a grave,   780
their greatness shines—deathless.

Better to win with no stain of dishonor   *antistrophe*
than to overthrow justice by violent means,
or the odious uses of power.
When mortals learn they can triumph
over justice, the victory's
sweet for a moment, but then
it withers and reproaches the guilty,
soon bringing disgrace to his house.
This is the life that I praise and esteem,   790
the life to which I aspire
—to wield no power in public or private
that goes beyond justice's bounds.

O aged son of Aeacus,   *epode*
I have no doubt the story is true
that you took up your glorious spear

and fought with the Lapiths against the Centaurs,
that you stood on the deck of the Argo then,
passing through dangerous waters,
the Crashing Rocks, sailing on to your   800
fame where the Symplegades front
the roiling sea. And when on that earlier day
Zeus's son brought great Troy
within the snare of his slaughtering net,
you, too, came back to Europe in triumph.

Enter HERMIONE'S NURSE.

NURSE   My dear women, today evil has followed
every evil. The mistress of this house,
Hermione—she is there within—has been
deserted by her father, and now, conscience-
stricken, she's awakened to what a dreadful deed   810
she's done in planning to kill Andromache
and her little son. She wants to die.
She fears her husband, fears expulsion from
this house, disgrace, and even that she herself
may be killed because she tried to take these lives
she had no right to take. She put her head
inside the noose and her servants barely saved her;
when later she took up the sword, they pried it from
her right hand. She's full of regret after
the fact and anguished over her wrongful deeds.   820
Friends, I'm tired of saving her from herself.
You try to save her now. Maybe
she'll be willing to listen to newcomers.

CHORUS   Listen, the servants are shouting in confirmation.
And now this pathetic woman will show us
just how sorry she is to have done what she did.
She leaves the house, running away from her servants'
grasp because she wants to die.

HERMIONE *enters and sings and dances about the stage.*
The NURSE *remains stationary and replies with*
spoken dialogue.

HERMIONE Misery, misery   *strophe*
          I'll tear my hair   830
          and furrow my cheeks with my nails.

    NURSE My child—what are you doing? Will you so disfigure
               yourself?

HERMIONE O lacey veil—go down to hell,   *antistrophe*
          stripped from my hair—into the wind!

    NURSE Child, cover your breasts, fasten your gown.

HERMIONE My gown can cover my breasts,   *strophe*
          but bare are the deeds I have done;
          my crimes are clear in my husband's eyes.

    NURSE You cry because, behind his back, you schemed
               this murder?

HERMIONE Grieving and grieving over my deeds   *antistrophe*   840
          my murderous daring, my plotting then—
          and now I'm accursed in all men's eyes.

    NURSE Your husband will forgive you.

HERMIONE Why did you pry the sword from my hand?
          Give it back, my friend, I'll strike my heart.
          Why do you keep me from the waiting noose?

    NURSE But what if I do let you go, crazy girl,
          to kill yourself?

HERMIONE Oh misery, my fate. Where is the dear
          flame for me? Where is the rock   850
          that I might climb, then plunge
          into the sea or the mountainous wood,
          into the care of the gods of the dead?

    NURSE Why grieve on and on?
          The gods send bad fortune
          to each of us, sooner or later.

HERMIONE Oh father you have left me
　　　　　alone on the shore.
　　　　　Father, you've left me desolate,
　　　　　without an oar—and now he will kill me,   860
　　　　　kill me! I'll no longer dwell
　　　　　in the house where I was a bride.
　　　　　To what god's statue shall I run?
　　　　　Shall I, like a slave, clasp the knees of a slave?
　　　　　How I wish I were a dark-winged bird,
　　　　　that I could soar far from Phthia,
　　　　　or that I were that pine-planked ship
　　　　　that sailed through the Symplegades.

NURSE I didn't like it when you committed crimes
　　　against the Trojan woman and I can't   870
　　　approve of you now that you are crazed with fear.
　　　Your husband will not throw off his ties to you.
　　　He won't be won over by the abusive speech
　　　of a barbarian. You are no Trojan prisoner of war,
　　　taken as a prize. You've brought a large dowry;
　　　you are a noble's daughter from a prosperous city.
　　　Your father will never abandon you
　　　or allow you to be thrown from this house.
　　　Come now, go inside. Don't make a spectacle
　　　of yourself in front of the palace. You will   880
　　　be disgraced, showing yourself out here.

HERMIONE *retreats toward the exit.*

CHORUS Look, here comes a foreigner, a stranger;
　　　　he's walking toward us in a great hurry.

Enter ORESTES.

ORESTES Women, strangers, is this the dwelling
　　　　of Achilles' son, his royal palace?

CHORUS It is, but who are you who asks?

ORESTES I am the son of Agamemnon
　　　　and Clytemnestra—my name is Orestes.
　　　　Traveling to the oracle of Zeus at Dodona, I've stopped

here in Phthia to ask after   890
my cousin, Hermione of Sparta, if she's
doing well. For though she dwells
so far from me, she's dear to my heart.

HERMIONE *comes forward to Orestes.*

HERMIONE O, you who have appeared, like a haven that shelters
the storm-tossed sailors, Agamemnon's son—
kneeling, I beg you, pity me whose distress you can see.
I wrap my arms, like wool-draped branches,
about your knees in wreaths of supplication.

ORESTES Oh—what is this? Am I mistaken, or is this
Menelaus's daughter, who should be queen here?   900

HERMIONE Yes, surely I am his daughter—the only daughter
whom Tyndareus's daughter Helen bore him
in their house.

ORESTES Oh Phoebus, healer, spare us such sorrow.
What is the matter? Do gods or men oppress you?

HERMIONE I'm to blame, but so is my husband, and so, too,
is a god partly at fault. I am undone, utterly undone.

ORESTES You have no children and so the trouble you have
must arise from your marriage bed.

HERMIONE That is my problem. You prompt me exactly.

ORESTES Is your husband in love with some other woman?   910

HERMIONE Yes, his captive prize—Hector's wife.

ORESTES One man with two loves—a disaster!

HERMIONE You see the problem. I sought my own solution.

ORESTES Did you weave the sorts of plots that women weave?

HERMIONE Yes, I plotted to kill her and her bastard son.

ORESTES And did you, or were you somehow thwarted?

HERMIONE Old Peleus stopped me, honoring that worthless pair.

ORESTES And did anyone help you in your attempt?

HERMIONE My father, who came from Sparta to help me.

ORESTES And did the old man get the better of him?   920

HERMIONE He was ashamed—and then he left me alone.

ORESTES I see. You fear your husband because of the things you
        have done.

HERMIONE It's true; he will kill me, and within his rights.
        What more can I say? I beg you, in the name
        of Kindred Zeus, take me from here—to the ends
        of the earth or to my father's house! The very
        walls seem to have taken a voice and say, "Go,"
        and all of Phthia hates me. If my husband
        leaves the oracle of Phoebus and finds me here
        when he arrives, he'll kill me most shamefully.   930
        Or else I'll become a slave to his concubine, who was
            once my slave.

            HERMIONE *pauses, looks off into the distance, and*
                          continues dreamily.

        How did I go so wrong? Now I see
        that I was spoiled by the gossip of my visitors,
        how I swelled with the flattery of those bad women!
        They said, "Why do you let this wretched slave
        share your husband's bed? I swear by Hera—
        in my house, if she enjoyed my husband,
        that would be the last of her pleasures!"
        I listened to these Sirens' words, the chatter
        of these cunning deceivers, and swelled with folly.   940
        Why did I spy so jealously on my husband
        when in fact I had everything I could want?
        I had wealth and full control of the house.
        I would have carried legitimate children while her

little bastards would grow up to be their slaves.
Never, never—it can't be said too often—
should a husband who has any sense
let women visit his wife in her house.
They can found a school of evil. One will
gain from the corruption of the bride; another,   950
a fallen woman herself, wants a companion
in vice. Others thrive on titillation.
This is the source of disease in a house.
Post a guard and bolt the gates and doors!
For women who come calling from outside
bring no good—only trouble.

CHORUS   Your own tongue is running on against
your own kind. The reasons are understandable, yet
women should use cosmetics to cover women's diseases.

ORESTES It is true that it is wise to listen to accounts   960
from the enemy camp. For I had heard a great
deal about the chaos in the house and the struggle
between you and the wife of Hector. I watched
        and waited
to see if you would want to stay here or if,
in terror over your murder of the slave woman,
you would want to escape this house.
Although it was not at your bidding that I came,
I hoped that by talking, as we are doing now,
I could take you away from this place.
You were to be my rightful wife—it was only   970
because of your father's treachery that you married
        this man.
Before the attack on Troy, he gave you to me.
And then he promised you to your present husband
if he would take the city. When Achilles' son came
home to this land, I forgave your father, but begged
Neoptolemus to relinquish his marriage plans,
I told of my family's misfortunes, my present fate,
        my terrible
exile, and how I could only marry a kinswoman.
But he turned to me with insults about
my mother's murder and the Furies' bloody eyes.   980
Crushed by the fate of my family,

crushed by my grief in being robbed of you,
I was forced against my will to leave you,
abandoning my plans. But now, since your own
fortunes have changed—since you, too, have fallen
into disaster, I will take you away
and restore you to your father.
Blood is a strong and powerful bond and when trouble
comes, there is no stronger ally than family.

HERMIONE Arranging marriages for me is my father's concern;   990
it's not up to me to make such a decision.
But, quickly, help me to leave this house
before my husband arrives and catches me—
and before old Peleus learns of my escape
and follows on horseback in hot pursuit.

ORESTES Don't worry about an old man. And have
no fear of Achilles' son, who insulted me.
Such a death trap I have set for him—
an immovable snare, right in the middle of his path.
I've wrought it with cunning and will speak no more
        of it,   1000
but the cliff of Delphi will know when it springs!
Oh, I'm "the matricide"! If my allies at Delphi
keep their oath, I'll teach him not to marry
one who belongs to me. And he'll be sorry
that he asked the god for satisfaction
for the death of his father. Yet his apology and
reparation to the god will be no use.
Thanks to Apollo and my own slanders, he'll
learn in death what my hatred is like. He'll taste
the god's enmity. The god turns his enemies   1010
upside down and will not allow their pride.

                        Exeunt ORESTES *and* HERMIONE.

CHORUS Phoebus, who walled in the high hill of Troy,   *strophe*
and Poseidon, you who drive your chariot
drawn by your storm-gray mares
over the storm-gray sea,
what violent anger made you dishonor
the work of your own hands, and give

it all over to to spear-loving Ares?
Troy into ruins—Troy into
ruins—how could you   1020
bear to bring such undoing?

On the plains of the Simois you yoked   *antistrophe*
fine horses, setting so many
contests of men, games of death
with no victor's garlands.
Wasted and gone are the kings of Ilium.
No more do the fires burn
there for the gods on the altars of Troy.
No more does the smoke go up there.

Gone is the son of Atreus,   *strophe* 1030
struck by the hand of his wife.
And dead and gone, too, is she—
struck down by the god at the hands of her children.
Spoken from god were the words the oracle
sent to Agamemnon's son.
Coming from Argos, he begged at the inmost
shrine—he the mother slayer. Oh God,
Oh Phoebus—how can I believe it?

So many women in so many plazas   *antistrophe*
of Greece then sang dirges for miserable sons.   1040
And so many wives left their homes
to go to the beds of strangers.
Not on you and not on yours alone
have fallen the grinding griefs.
Greece, too, suffered a plague.
It swooped out of Phrygia,
onto the placid and fertile fields,
raining down bloody death.

Enter PELEUS.

PELEUS Women of Phthia, answer my question.
A vague report's arrived that Menelaus's   1050
daughter has left the house and gone away.
I've hurried here to learn if this is true.

For those of us at home should mind
the cares of those we love who are abroad.

CHORUS   All that you've heard is true. I have
a duty to tell you the troubles I've witnessed.
The Queen has left this house in flight.

PELEUS   Fearing what? Tell me the story.

CHORUS   She feared her husband—that he might expel her.

PELEUS   Because of her plot to kill the boy?   1060

CHORUS   Yes, and her plot to kill the slave woman.

PELEUS   Did she leave with her father? Who was with her?

CHORUS   Agamemnon's son came and took her away.

PELEUS   And what was his aim? To marry her?

CHORUS   Yes, and he plans to kill your grandson.

PELEUS   By lurking in ambush or in a fair fight, face to face?

CHORUS   In Loxias's sacred shrine, with the help of Delphians.

PELEUS   Oh, dreaded news! Quick, someone go
in haste to the holy hall at Delphi and tell
what has happened here. Go, before   1070
Achilles' son is murdered by his enemies!

Enter MESSENGER.

MESSENGER   Terrible news I bring you. It's a curse to bear such tidings
to you, old sir—to you and any who love my master.

PELEUS   Oh, my prophetic heart senses disaster!

MESSENGER   The news I bear is that the son of your son is dead—
Old man, so many strokes he took from swords—
the swords of Delphians and the Mycenean stranger.

CHORUS Oh, oh, steady there, old sir.
        Hold steady there.

PELEUS I'm done, destroyed — my voice is gone, my limbs cannot
              hold me.   1080

CHORUS Hang on, something may be possible.
        Listen, hold yourself together.

PELEUS Fate has overwhelmed me at the final
        verge of life. I am so unhappy!
        How did the only son of my only son perish?
        An unbearable story that I must hear.

MESSENGER When we arrived in Phoebus's famous land,
        we walked about for three full days,
        taking in the sights, seeing all there was
        to see. But this caused suspicion.   1090
        The citizens who dwell there kept forming
        little knots of talk. And Orestes ranged
        through the town, whispering a slander in every ear:
        "Keep watch on this man," he said, "he roams about
        the sacred way where the gold brims in our treasuries.
        Maybe he's come back a second time
        to complete his earlier plan and ransack
        the temple of Phoebus." And so rumor seethed
        throughout the city. The magistrates gathered
        in the council chambers and those who guarded   1100
        the god's treasury posted watches within
        the colonnades. We, still knowing
        nothing of this, took our sheep, raised on
        Parnassus's pastures, and went before
        the altars, taking our place beside the Delphian
        agents and priests. Then someone said, "Young man
        what should we ask of the god? What do you desire?"
        And he answered, "Only to make reparation for
        my earlier sin against Apollo, when once
        I demanded satisfaction for my father's blood."   1110
        But Orestes' story reigned —
        All believed my master was lying and bent
        to some foul purpose. My master then mounted
        to the temple to pray to Phoebus at the altars

before the inner shrine. But all at once
there rose, out of the shadows cast by the laurels,
armed men who had been lying in ambush—
Clytemnestra's son had contrived it all.
Neoptolemus in plain sight was praying,
then they, armed with whetted swords, unseen,   1120
stabbed the unarmored son of Achilles.
He backed away, he wasn't wounded deeply;
he drew his sword and snatched some votive armor
that hung on pegs on the temple wall; he took
his stand at an altar; turning his terrible face
toward them, he shouted to Delphi's sons, "Why
do you want to kill me when I come in piety?
Why am I being sent to death?" And though
there were many gathered there, not one
spoke—instead they pelted him with stones   1130
that fell like hail about him. He used his armor
as a shield and held the shield itself
now here, now there, and back again. But all
to no avail. The attackers pressed with their arsenal:
arrows, javelins, altar forks and knives
for sacrifice came flying all about him.
You could have seen his Pyrrhic dance as he
stepped and sprung, dodging their weapons.
Soon they circled and penned him in until
he could hardly breathe, but he left the animal   1140
accepting altar and with that famous leap
that Troy had known—he charged upon them.
Like doves facing a hawk, they turned and fled
in panic. Many fell, jammed into the gateway—
fell from his sword and by crushing each other.
In that holy place an unholy clamor rose,
echoing against the stone. Then calm for a moment
while my master stood still, his armor gleaming
in a shaft of sunlight—from deep within the temple
a dreadful voice, bloodcurdling, roused them back   1150
to attack. And that was when Achilles'
son collapsed, killed by a Delphian who,
stepping out from the pack, stabbed him
through the ribs with a blade. When
he fell to earth, were there any in that
throng who did not then go on to strike him?

With rock and sword they bruised and rent every inch
of his beautiful body. His body lay near an altar
in the incense-filled temple. They tossed it outside.
We gathered it up and hurried back to you,   1160
old sir, so you could mourn and bury him.
This is how the god who prophesies for all,
who judges morality for all mankind, has treated
the son of Achilles when he came to make amends.
Like a cowardly man, he brooded on
old quarrels—how can we call that wise?

Enter a procession carrying NEOPTOLEMUS' *body.*

CHORUS Oh now look, how our Lord arrives home
on a litter, his body is carried from Delphi.
How wretched is he, how unlucky. And you
are the same, a poor luckless old man   1170
who must welcome Achilles' son in this way.
This was not what you hoped for and now
you yourself share this same cursed fate.

PELEUS *becomes the chief mourner, singing a lament. The*
CHORUS *responds.*

PELEUS Misery! What a disaster I see here   *strophe*
before me and take into my arms and into my house.
What sad sorrow, alas! I am finished.
I'm done for, undone!
Oh sad Thessalian city!
Finished now, none of my race survives,
no children left in the halls of my house!   1180
Oh how wretched I am from misfortune!
To whom can I turn for consoling?
Oh face that I love so, and poor knees and hands!
Better some god had killed you long ago
on the banks of the Simois at Troy.

CHORUS Yes, then laurels would be his—
and you would now be less miserable.

PELEUS Marriage, oh marriage, that ruined my house   *antistrophe*
and laid waste to my city!

Alas, my poor child, my poor family!   1190
Never should we have embraced that vile union;
Hermione cast death on our house and our home.
Oh what evil she brought to the son of my son.
Better to perish by lightning and thunder
than yoke yourself firm to disaster.
How I still wish you, a mortal,
had never accused the great god Phoebus
of killing your father by Paris's murderous arrow.

CHORUS Oh grief! I must lament   *strophe*
        my lord now with the song,   1200
        the keen we sing the dead.

PELEUS Oh grief! so old and luckless now,
        I take up the lament.

CHORUS It was a god who caused
        this doom. It was a god
        who made this disaster.

PELEUS Dear child, you've left me desolate
        you've left the house bereft—
        all children gone and me alone.

CHORUS You should have died before your children.   1210

PELEUS I want to rend my hair.
        I want to strike my head
        with savage hands. Oh city see
        how Phoebus twice robbed me of my sons!

CHORUS Old man, you've known such grief,   *antistrophe*
        you've suffered through such pain.
        What afterlife awaits you?

PELEUS No child, no help, no stop to suffering—
        unending misery to my dying day.

CHORUS In vain did the gods bless you in your marriage.   1220

PELEUS My blessing's flown—
        gone far beyond the reach of boasts!

CHORUS Alone in a lonely house.

PELEUS I've lost my city—gone!
   I'll throw my scepter down!
   And you, daughter of Nereus, who dwell in the cave
     of night,
   will see me here fallen in ruin.

CHORUS Yet now—look! What movement do I see?
    What holy thing?
   Women, come and see! What marvel—look!
   Something divine comes among us, on the white air; 1230
   it rides on the wind and appears shimmering here
   on the grass of our horse-pasturing Phthia!

   THETIS *enters, elevated on a machine, and alights in front*
               of the temple.

THETIS Peleus, it is Thetis. Because we shared the marriage bed,
   I've left the house of Nereus to come to you
   —to say first do not give way too much
   to the sorrows that burden you now. For I, too,
   who never should have borne children who would perish,
   since I am a goddess and the daughter of a god,
   have lost our child, Achilles, fleetest of foot
   and noblest of the Greeks. Listen to why I have come: 1240
   go now, take the slain son of Achilles to
   Delphi's altar. Bury him there, a reproach
   to the Delphians, so that his tomb may proclaim that
   he was brutally killed by the hand of Orestes. Then send
   the captive woman, Andromache, to settle in the land
   of the Molossians and marry Helenus.
   Her son, too, the last of the line of Aeacus,
   will settle there and his sons, an unbroken
   line of kings, will bestow to Molossia
   their blessed, prosperous, rule. For, old sir, 1250
   your race and mine will not be laid waste
   as it may now seem. Nor is Troy
   destroyed. For Troy, too, is in the gods'
   care, though it fell by the will of Athene.
   As for you, because you should be glad
   for your marriage to me, I will set you free

from mortal sorrow and make you a god—
you will never know death or decay.
And we shall dwell, as a god and goddess, in the house
of Nereus from this time until forever.   1260
There, as you walk, dry-shod, out
of the depths of the sea, you will find your son and mine,
Achilles, living in his island home,
Leuke, amid the Euxine Sea.
Go now to the sacred city of Delphi, take
the body of this man. And when he is laid in the earth,
go to the hollow cave where Sepias rises
from the water and sit and wait in that place
where the cuttlefish swim. Wait until I rise from
the waves with my chorus of fifty Nereids to call you.   1270
All this is fated; it is the will of Zeus.
Cease now, cease your grieving.
Death is the judgment that stands over mortals.
Death is the debt that each must pay.

> *Exit* THETIS *on the machine.*

PELEUS Oh lady, oh noble companion who once shared
my bed, daughter of Nereus, farewell! Your plans
do honor to yourself and your children. I shall put
aside my sorrow at your bidding, goddess.
When I have buried this man, I shall go to the glens
of Pelion where I took your beauty in my arms.   1280
Shall a man not seek a noble wife
or give his daughter to a man of high birth?
And should a man not avoid an unworthy
match, even if she brings a large dowry?
Then the gods will not send ill will.

> *Exeunt all while the* CHORUS *chants.*

CHORUS The gods appear in many forms.
We cannot know their ends.
What we cannot dream unfolds
and what we dream will vanish.
Such was the outcome of this story.   1290

NOTES ON THE TEXT

All stage directions are supplied by W. Smith and are simply inferences from the text.

THE SCENE

The temple is center stage in this play, I think, despite the fact that the more common scenic arrangement was that of palace entrance as the central feature. The ritual of supplication that Euripides invokes with Andromache's initial posture is well described already in the *Iliad* and *Odyssey*, the oldest Greek archaic literature, and the ritual persists virtually unchanged throughout antiquity. The suppliant put him or herself in a sacred place (Cassandra and Priam both sought altars at the sack of Troy, Odysseus sought the hearth in Scheria), declaring him or herself under the protection of the god. To supplicate a human being's protection or kindness, the suppliant took a humble position at the person's feet and tried to encircle his/her knees, and/or take hold of his beard to make more binding the obligation of the person to whom he/she was appealing. It was dangerous for those supplicated to offend the god by rejecting such supplication. Zeus Hikesios was the high god of the Greeks in his role of protector of all suppliants.

1ff The prologue (technically everything before the entrance of the chorus) consists of Andromache's monologue, a dramatic scene between Andromache and the maidservant, and Andromache's lament. Her memories of Thebe, her birthplace and place of childhood joy, recall allusively a rich strain in archaic poetry that celebrated her marriage to Hector, including a lavish procession from Thebe to Troy. By chance, the only narrative poem by Sappho that has been preserved (in fragments only) describes the homecoming of Hector with his bride Andromache (Sappho 44). Such lyric poetry from the Aegean presents a backdrop for Athenian tragedy's treatment of related themes.

15 *islander Neoptolemus* For his birth on Scyros, see the Glossary. The significance of "islander" here is not clear, but the audience might hear it as a disparagement: he is from the outlands, not a sophisticate. Neoptolemus' violent nature (see, e.g., the description of him in *Aeneid* 2) is somewhat played down in this play, though in the *Andromache*'s version of his story he impetuously went to Delphi to demand satisfaction from Apollo for the death of his father, and at the play's opening has left Andromache alone because he has repented his brashness and has gone to Delphi again to ask the god's forgiveness.

103ff Andromache's lament is in elegiac meter. It is the only elegy in what remains of Greek tragedy. Elegiac verse was used for many purposes in archaic poetry: love poetry, philosophical moralizing, marching songs, etc., as well as for tombstone inscriptions, which probably gave the meter its reputation as a rhythm for mourning.

117ff The chorus of Phthian women. Fifteen members make up the chorus. One chorus member, the leader, speaks for the chorus in dialogue. The whole chorus dances and sings, probably in unison, in performing the choral odes between the acts. The lyric portions of the play, those sung to musical accompaniment, are generally divided into strophes and antistrophes (movements and answering movements) that signal repeated rhythmical passages. Probably the music and dance shared the repetition.

126, 138 "Know thyself," *gnothi sauton*, was inscribed at the temple at Delphi, part of the moralizing advice that came from that shrine. The phrase, much quoted and alluded to throughout Greek antiquity, was generally taken to mean be aware of your mortality and your limitations. (William Arrowsmith's comments on what he calls modality, in his translation of *Alcestis* in this series, are illuminating on this subject.) Here the chorus's extension to "know your limits as woman, slave, barbarian" fits the usage. It is almost inevitable in heroic literature that someone so advised will do the opposite, and Andromache is being characterized as heroic.

155 *License . . . to speak* Eleutherostomia, the right to speak one's mind, was a precious value to the Athenians, for which they thanked their laws and constitution. Euripides acknowledges it frequently. Here, Hermione

seems to be suggesting that her dowry, which would go back home with her if she were divorced, is what assures her status in Phthia, and her right to self-assertion.

282 It is perhaps striking that the same term is used here for the goddesses' quarrel as for the strife between Andromache and Hermione, *eridi stugera*, hateful strife. Hesiod says that there is bad, but also good *eris*, for example, the hateful fighting between brothers for their inheritance, and the productive competition between shoemakers. Euripides did not have to have that in mind, though *eris* in the *Theogony* is called *stugere*. Euripides uses *eris* only twice more in this play, both times in the next choral ode: line 471 where it refers to the kinds of strife the chorus disapproves of, such as contests between two wives, and line 493 where it says Hermione is killing Andromache because of irrational *eris*. Thus, it appears, Euripides uses the word *eris* in this play with something specific in mind, something like the horrors that come out of sexual jealousy, and it appears that he is comparing the judgment of Paris, in the goddesses' contest for who is the fairest, with the contest of Hermione with Andromache. He does not dwell on the naked beauty the goddesses displayed, but on the viciousness of their dialogue to win the contest and on the trickery implicit in Cypris' promise.

313 *Enter Menelaus*. Staging of tragedies often implies nonspeaking characters, as here attendants for Menelaus. We have no ancient evidence to draw on for the traditions of staging in that regard but must make our inferences from the text of the play. Menelaus must have lackeys to support him, as later Peleus must have attendants to face them down.

369 The chorus traditionally intervenes verbally between long speeches, often counseling moderation or taking sides in argument. Greek playwrights must have found it a useful kind of transition.

420 *When you kiss your father, when he lifts you in his arms, tell him with your tears* Molossus' appearance here is suggestive of scenes in the *Iliad* that relate to Astyanax. Particularly poignant in the scene in *Iliad* 6, in which Andromache appeals to Hector not to let her become a widow and Astyanax an orphan, is Hector's approach to his baby while the baby shrinks from his fierce aspect, until he adjusts his war helmet to reveal his face, after which he lifts the baby in his arms to kiss him.

497 The chorus introduces this section in anapestic rhythm, which is not the meter of dialogue nor of lyric. Probably the anapests were chanted, half-sung,

with musical accompaniment. Andromache and Molossus sing a strophe and antistrophe in lyric meters. After each, Menelaus responds to them in anapests. The chorus in 547 resumes the spoken dialogue meter, iambic trimeter, for the Peleus scene.

530 *Plead with him* For the mode of formal suppliance see the note on line 1ff. Menelaus will evade Molossus here to keep him from touching his knees or beard.

629 *senseless slaughter* The reference is to Iphigeneia.

649ff For Peleus' father Aeacus and his reputation, see the Glossary. Menelaus alleges here that Peleus has betrayed the moral code of an international Greek aristocracy that makes its alliances by marriage. In raising this issue, Euripides is being historically accurate: there was such a nexus among the *aristoi*, the "best families" in Greek city states of the archaic period.

755 *Make sure . . . we are not ambushed* The roads of rural Greece were never safe from pirates, with the result that protection was always desirable. There were numerous shrines for seeking the gods' protection, and travelers used convoys whenever possible. Here, Andromache's fear that Menelaus could arrange an ambush is not unreasonable.

770 The saying "Better not to be born than to suffer. . . ." was a not uncommon poetic lead-in to descriptions of life's evils that are hard to face. Euripides offers a new version of it here. Initially one may wonder whom is the chorus thinking of? Peleus? Menelaus? Andromache? Their sentiment in 782ff, "Better to win with no stain of dishonor," is reminiscent of Pindar and others' praise of the athletic victors in epinician lyrics. Finally, the epode, 794ff, fulfills the ode and makes it clear that it is a victory ode for Peleus' career that the chorus has been singing.

829ff Hermione begins a lament, but the Nurse and the chorus, instead of joining and supporting the lament, reject it. For the form of lament see the note below on 1174ff.

889 *Traveling to the oracle of Zeus at Dodona* Phthia is not on the route to Dodona from anywhere Orestes is likely to have been. And his admission later (963ff) seems to indicate that he is being disingenuous here.

925 *Kindred Zeus* She invokes Zeus *homognios,* Zeus who oversees matters of kin-
ship. He would normally be worshipped by families, who would pray
to him to keep them together and make them prosper. He would also
have been invoked in reference to the special obligations to take vengeance for slights against the family.

978 *marry a kinswoman* Keeping wealth in the family was a major concern in marriage law and practice. The disgraced Orestes is not a great catch, but
the family is obligated to be concerned for him. Hermione's inheritance, for example, can be kept in the family if she marries her cousin.

1004 *he'll be sorry that he asked the god for satisfaction* Neoptolemus was accepting
and acting out the normal obligation of a kinsman to take vengeance
or get satisfaction for a family member's death or disgrace, in this case
saying that Apollo had murdered Achilles by guiding the arrow of Paris
to its mark. By demanding satisfaction from the god, Neoptolemus in
effect demanded reparation by a money payment or challenged the
god to a duel. Such a challenge to a god was obviously suicidally rash,
as the sequel proves.

1072 Peleus enters (1049) having heard that Hermione is gone. The messenger enters
immediately to tell him that Neoptolemus has been killed by Orestes'
plotting, and implies that Orestes was present at the death. But Orestes,
while he was onstage, said only that he had laid a plot to do away with
Neoptolemus, and implied that its execution was to come in the future
(996ff). Delphi is several days' journey from Phthia. Neoptolemus' body
arrives immediately after the messenger's news. There seem to be se-
rious inconsistencies here. It appears that Euripides did not establish a
"time line" of which he made the audience aware and to which he
adhered. Instead he chose inconsistency, stretching and compressing
time and distance. Orestes could hardly say to Hermione, "I've killed
your husband," without disjointing Euripides' emotional sequence.
And the Greek theater had no curtain to drop, or program to say "act
three, two weeks later." The inconsistencies are problematic if we di-
rect our attention to them, and Euripides keeps our attention off them,
or tries to. This is not unusual in Greek tragedy, the audience of which
was used to the convention that the choral odes could cover the passage
of an indeterminate amount of time.

1095 *treasuries* The sacred way approaching the temple was lined with treasury
buildings in which the various Greek cities stored and displayed their
dedications to Apollo. They took pride in the lavishness of the treasures.

1103 *took our sheep* The worshipers would buy perfect animals in the precinct of the temple and hand them over to the priests for sacrifice at the large altar in front of the temple, where the priests would offer prayers on behalf of the worshipers. Then Neoptolemus mounts the stairs of the temple alone to pray inside. At the top of the stairs is a porch supported by rows of columns. In the porch there are small altars, and on the wall of the temple itself dedicatory offerings are hung, including armor.

1137–40 *Pyrrhic dance . . . leap* This was a martial dance performed by men and boys in armor. Invention of the *pyrrhiche* was sometimes attributed to Achilles' passionate dance around Patroclus' pyre, but more often attributed to Neoptolemus (with a pun on his other name, Pyrrhus), "leaping" from the wooden horse or doing a victory dance after killing Eurypylus at Troy.

1174ff The lament. Formal lamentation (in life as well as art) was carried on by a chief mourner who stated the themes of his or her grief, and a supporting chorus of mourners who reinforced what the chief mourner said and suggested new themes. Here Peleus, the chief mourner, sings his grief in lyric verse and the chorus responds at first in dialogue, but by the second strophe joins in lyric song.

1230 *on the white air* The deus ex machina was brought on stage carried by a crane, which probably swiveled so as to raise her and bring her out from behind her own temple and set her down in front of it.

1267 *Sepias* A promontory near Iolchos, which is near to Phthia. In some traditions Peleus "wooed" Thetis there by catching hold of her when she came out of the Aegean and holding her tight while she went through various transformations (line 1280 below). Hence Peleus is to return to the place where he and Thetis had their first encounter.

1286ff This tailpiece appears at the end of *Alcestis, Helen, Bacchae,* and *Medea.* Like the theophany that precedes, the chorus's exit lines distance the audience from the emotion of the play by invoking a universal perspective, the notion of universal design, or at least of superhuman influence.

GLOSSARY

ACHILLES: The greatest warrior at Troy, hero of the *Iliad*. He was the
son of Peleus and Thetis and father of Neoptolemus. In mythology his father put him on the island of Scyros to save him
from service in the Trojan war. There he fathered Neoptolemus with the Nymph Deidameia, but Odysseus came to find
him and recruit him for the war.

AEACUS: King of Aegina, known for his piety. He was father to Peleus,
q.v.

AGAMEMNON: The supreme commander of the Greeks at Troy, murdered by his wife, Clytemnestra, on his return home.

ANDROMACHE: A Trojan woman, widow of Hector, slave and concubine of Neoptolemus.

APHRODITE: The goddess of love, daughter of Zeus and Dione. After
a quarrel had broken out at the wedding of Peleus and Thetis
among Aphrodite, Athene, and Hera about which of them was
the most beautiful, Hermes brought the goddesses to Mount
Ida for Paris to judge between them. Aphrodite won the contest by promising him Helen. (See the choral ode, 277ff.)

APOLLO: Son of Zeus and Leto, god of prophesy whose shrine at Delphi was acknowledged by the world in general. His oracle
announced that he officially supported Sparta in the war
against Athens, and would help Sparta however he could.

ARES: God of war, variously portrayed. Often he is a coward. As Ares' lover, Aphrodite is often asked in prayer to tame his destructiveness.

ATREUS: Father of Agamemnon and Menelaus.

CASSANDRA: Trojan princess who was beloved of Apollo and was made a prophetess by him. But when she scorned him, he cursed her so she would never be believed.

CENTAURS: A race of half horse-half man creatures which produced some wise teachers, including Chiron to whom Achilles was entrusted by Peleus and Thetis for his education. They also had a reputation for getting out of control: hence the story that they got drunk at the wedding of the Lapith king Pirithous, and tried to abduct the bride.

CYPRIS: A name for Aphrodite.

DELPHI: The location of Apollo's temple on Mt. Parnassus at which he prophesied through the medium of his priestess.

DODONA: The location of a famous oracle of Zeus in northwestern Greece.

ERINYES: Also Furies. Avenging spirits called forth by blood of murdered people. The Erinyes of his mother pursued Orestes. Apollo protected him and eventually purified him.

EUXINE SEA: The Greek name for the Black Sea. Euxine means "friendly to strangers," and is a euphemism for its real name, *axine*, "unfriendly to strangers."

HECTOR: The greatest Trojan hero in the *Iliad,* also portrayed as a man of sense in council and a conscientious husband and father. Eldest son of Priam and Hecuba, he was killed by Achilles after he had killed Patroclus.

HECUBA: Queen of Troy, in legend the mother of fifty children to Priam. Her grief figured widely in Greek literature, including Euripides' *Hecuba* and *Trojan Women.*

HELEN: The most beautiful woman in the world, wife of Menelaus, mother of Hermione. Many Greek heroes were her suitors, and swore to help her chosen husband if needed. Thus the Greek contingent to the Trojan War when she was stolen by Paris.

HELENUS: Brother of Hector who ended up as king of Molossia. Andromache is betrothed to him by Thetis at the end of the play. Their menage is visited by Aeneas in *Aeneid* Bk 3.

HERMIONE: Spartan princess, daughter of Helen and Menelaus. She was married to Neoptolemus, but in Euripides' version and others, previously promised to Orestes by Menelaus.

ILIUM: Troy.

LACEDAIMON: Sparta.

MENELAUS: King of Sparta. His story is told in the *Iliad* and *Odyssey*. In the *Iliad* he is, if not cowardly, of somewhat limited courage and skill in generalship. In the *Odyssey* he is a gracious knight at home in Sparta.

MOLOSSIA: A small kingdom in Epirus, in northwestern Greece, with a long tradition of independence. Molossus, Andromache's son, is considered the head of the dynasty, which called itself Aeacids.

MOLOSSUS: Son of Neoptolemus and Andromache in the tradition. Euripides ignores other aspects of the tradition that speak of children of Neoptolemus and Hermione.

NEOPTOLEMUS: Son of Achilles, born on Scyros (see Achilles above) and therefore called Islander. He was summoned to the Trojan war after Achilles' death, as the one who, according to prophecy, was needed to capture Troy. In myth, he was the one who killed Priam.

NEREUS, NEREID: Nereus was a sea god, famous in myth for his cleverness. His sea-nymph daughters are called Nereids, of whom Thetis is one.

ORESTES: Son of Agamemnon and Clytemnestra, Menelaus' nephew, cousin of Hermione. He was pursued by furies (Erinyes) after he killed his mother to avenge his father.

PARIS: A royal prince of Troy, he was made a shepherd because of his mother's ominous dream that he would destroy Troy. The three goddesses came to him to have their beauty judged, and he judged Aphrodite the fairest when she promised him Helen. He killed Achilles with an arrow at the siege of Troy.

PELEUS: King of Phthia, father of Achilles by Thetis, and grandfather of Neoptolemus. His father Aeacus was king of Aegina. Myths related that Peleus had to leave Aegina because he and his brother Telamon killed their half-brother Phocus because of jealousy of his athletic prowess. Pindar, Nem. 5 speaks of his exile, and of his subsequent career of virtue that led Zeus to choose him as the mortal who would marry Thetis. Many stories are recorded of his adventures, which are also a frequent subject in archaic art. The choral ode 770ff recalls his participation in the battle of the Lapiths and Centaurs, the voyage after the Golden Fleece, and the first sack of Troy.

PHOEBUS: An epithet of Apollo.

PHRYGIA: An area of northwestern Turkey, of which in mythology the Trojans were the leading people.

PHTHIA: Also called Phthiotis. A region of east central Thessaly, the kingdom of Achilles in the *Iliad*.

POSEIDON: Brother of Zeus and Hades, god of earthquakes, horses, and especially the sea.

PRIAM: King of Troy. In myth he was killed at an altar by Neoptolemus, but that story is ignored in *Andromache*.

SIMOIS: River that runs through the plain of Troy.

SPARTA: The major city of the central Peloponnesus, home of Menelaus and Helen.

SYMPLEGADES: Clashing rocks that the Argonauts had to pass to enter the Hellespont.

THEBE: The city Thebe, birthplace of Andromache and of Chryse, is described in the *Iliad*. It was on the foothills of Mt. Ida, south of Troy and was destroyed by the Greek army.

THESSALY: Thessaly is the largest and most important agricultural district of Greece. It is in the center of Greece, with Mt. Olympus on the north, the Aegean sea on the east, and Mt. Oeta on the south.

THETIS: A sea goddess, married to Peleus because, as Zeus discovered, she was destined to bear a son greater than his father. A shrine to her would be called a Thetideion.

TROY: The classic portrayal of Troy in the *Iliad*, a city on a hill besieged for ten years by the united Greeks, was followed in other literary works. Archaeology has confirmed many details.

ZEUS: The supreme god of the Greeks, protector of guest-friends and suppliants. In the *Iliad* Zeus accedes to Thetis' request to turn the war against the Greeks to revenge the slight to Achilles' honor.